Th… Nova Scotia

Canoeing, camping and coping in the backwoods

Bud Inglis

NIMBUS
PUBLISHING LTD

Nimbus Publishing Limited
PO Box 9301, Station A
Halifax, NS B3K 5N5
(902) 455-4286

Design: Joan Sinclair
Line drawing illustrations: Bud Inglis
Front cover photo: Ivan Robicheau; back cover: Briant Burgess

Printed and bound in Canada

Canadian Cataloguing in Publication Data
Inglis, Bud
Through deepest Nova Scotia
ISBN 1-55109-233-6
1. Nova Scotia—Description and travel. 2. Inglis, Bud. I. Title.

FC2317.5. I65 1999 917.1604'4 C99-950030-9
FC1037. I65 1999

Nimbus Publishing acknowledges the financial support of the Canada Council and the Department of Canadian Heritage.

Table of Contents

PART ONE

A journey from the Sissiboo to the Shelburne River, and out to Lake Rossignol

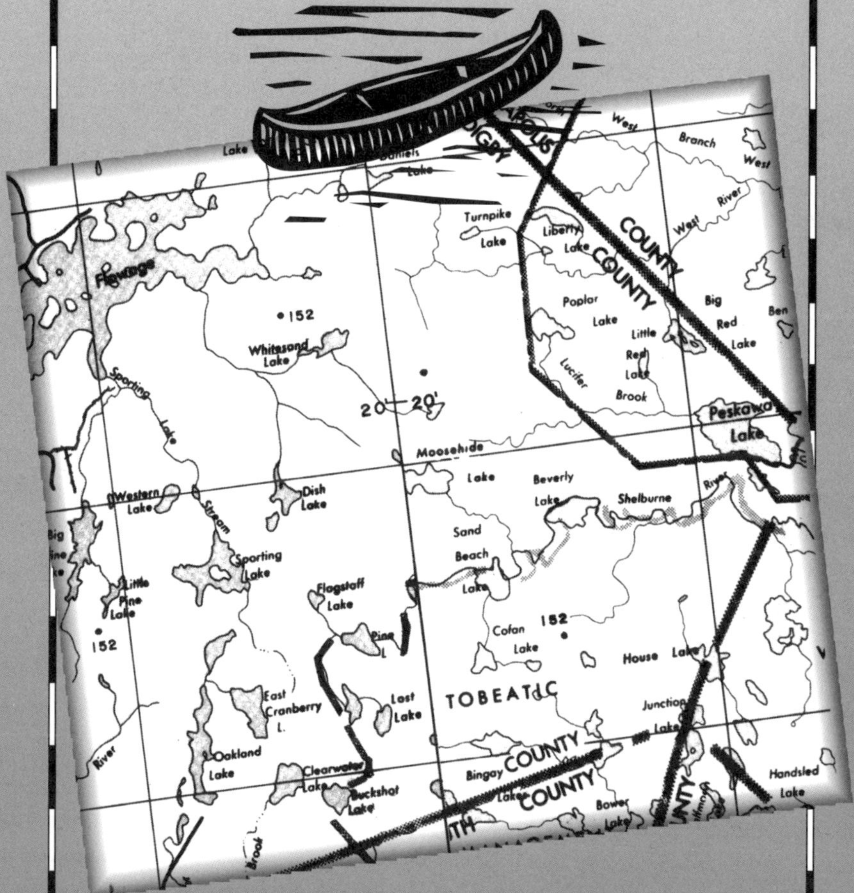

Not a very bright idea!

Suddenly you get the idea that you'd like to do something different from what you've been doing for the past several decades. All that woods travel—getting to favourite fishing spots, lugging heavy loads, blazing trails on snowshoes, or winching your vehicle out of damn near impossible holes—you now look at with a jaded eye. Why not a change of venue? Why not face a new challenge? You've done that other stuff for so long, you've got it down pat. Instead of marking time why not just keep on moving until you've seen the remotest, most pristine country available?

Of course that would mean travelling by canoe and carrying the slimmest amount of gear practicable—no outboard motors and gasoline, or the fishing gear you always had too much of. This would be the real test of how well you can get along in the woods. You're beginning to get excited about the idea.

This is almost the twenty-first century so you can't expect to be like a Samuel Hearne or a Titus Smith in Nova Scotia. You can't live the awesome months-long-foot-slogging-under-the-most-trying-fraught-with-danger conditions endured by those geographical surveyors of eighty or so years ago, who were the most intrepid, hardy examples of fine manhood you could find at the time. No, you're just a romantic dreamer, who, if the truth be known, is not up for the great physical exploits undertaken by those men whom you pretend to want to copy. So just do what's within your scope and leave it at that. Well, where to go?

For its size, Nova Scotia attracts a surprisingly high number of sportsmen. But up until the 1930s, it was a mecca to the visiting sport. It had a reputation of offering just about the finest trout fishing anywhere, and that went for the hunting of moose and caribou as well, although caribou were scarce by the turn of the century. This implies lots of deep woods and countless lakes and streams—and that's what the sport got. Now, despite the fact that Nova Scotia has the lowest ratio (25 per cent) of provincial Crown land to total land area in Canada, with the exception of P.E.I., it still has some very remote areas, which, it appears, the provincial government is committed to maintaining in their wild state. So let's traverse the longest, wildest route left in the province, where no roads probe and where the moose still range.

* * *

The preliminaries start slowly, but they fuel the hankering to plant that first foot on the trail. Doug and I pour over the topographical map on the table, either his finger or mine pointing and tracing the route. Boy, this is some easy! You just go here then you go along there; you carry here and paddle along there; and the first thing you know you're out here! Looks simple enough. It's not like we are a couple of trailblazers. We know that others have done this adventurous route we are studying. If they could do it then so could we.

Still, two guys like us bracketing sixty would do well to consider the youthfulness and physical condition of our predecessors on this chosen route. And they knew the equipment they needed for their sojourn. They were young and smart. We refrained from telling ourselves that we'd been travelling the woods for years and knew what had to be done. "Remember our age," we thought, and "compare the springiness of our bones to those youngsters."

While we were studying the map one of us insisted that there were to be no physical heroics. None of that heavy bulling we normally did, making just one carry-in to where we'd be until we were ready to come out. No, this was serious business and not just the usual fun jaunt where you took in a jar of this, a tin of that, and a bottle of something else. This was now a matter of efficiency—in everything we would be doing on the trip. If we wanted to retrace the footfalls of our predecessors to a happy conclusion, we had better watch ourselves.

There was one question that haunted us although neither of us made the least mention of it; we probably didn't want to spook each other. But was it sensible to be travelling through forty-eight miles of wilderness when one of us could break a leg or have a heart attack? What could the other guy do? He couldn't carry his buddy over such a long distance. If he took off alone for help, it could take days. Likely one of us would end up dead. Those earlier travellers in two or three canoes would have been able to cope with a like situation. But we would be travelling alone just like Titus Smith and those other indomitable government surveyors.

We were pretty well agreed on the choice of a canoe. We certainly weren't going to use a canvas-covered cedar canoe what with all the rapids we were going to have to run. And an aluminum canoe was out of the question. We had had our fill of aluminum boats and canoes grinding to a halt on some submerged granite boulder; oh how that aluminum fetches up on rough surfaces! The only feasible choice would be fibreglass or some polymer material—something that would keep sliding along those sharp cutting edges of the granite, and let the canoe continue on its way. That we could arrange.

Scrimping, with two stoves

The Shelburne River doesn't even pass through Shelburne County. It begins at Buckshot Lake in Digby County, passes into Queens County, and empties out into Lake Rossignol. It's located in the remotest part of the province, but there is more remote country to the west of Buckshot Lake, and we wanted to take in this area as well. We wanted to see the whole of the remotest territory left in Nova Scotia. That meant we'd have to put our canoe in at Sporting Lake Stream, close to where it enters Fifth Lake (Sissiboo Flowage), work our way south through five lakes, then into Buckshot Lake and the headwaters of the Shelburne.

Having mapped our route, we concentrated on what the military calls "logistics." Since we would be coming out 130 miles (by car), from where we went in, we had to arrange with friends who had a couple of vehicles, to take us in to the starting point, and leave a vehicle at the destination point on Lake Rossignol.

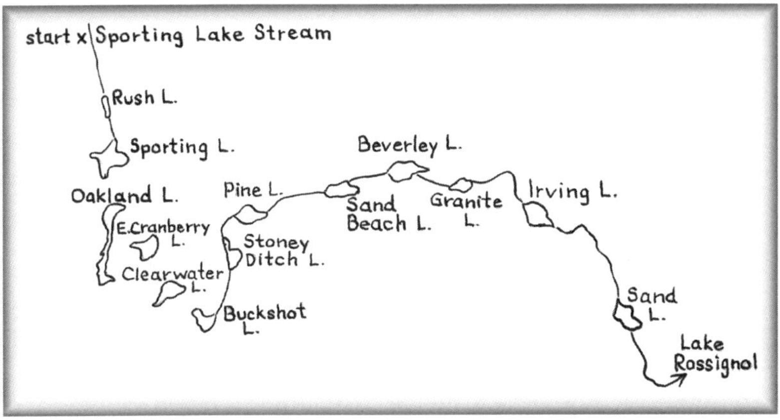

Next came the important chore of assembling equipment and food. Alone, you are bound to overlook something so it's good to plan together. In our leisurely discussions of things to consider, three cardinal rules always presented themselves and in the same order: keep dry, keep warm, and bring enough food.

Keeping dry had never been at the top of the list for me. Whenever I got wet I could always dry out beside a nice open fire, or in front of a hot stove in a cabin. Getting wet was never more than a temporary inconvenience. Keeping my gear light and simple was always my first concern, so I scrimped on extra long underwear because of the nice fireplaces along the way. I was to learn a hard lesson here.

While we decided on our own clothing needs, we religiously checked with each other on food, cooking implements, and lighting. Doug would look after one thing, I another, and we were careful not to duplicate. Although this wasn't a fishing trip, I was to bring along a small, six-piece spinning rod with a few lures and flies just in case we needed to supplement our food supply. There was the thought that passing through miles and miles of pristine waters, the fishing just had to be great!

* * *

Food for a woods trip is a subject that can make for a lot of discussion, especially on a trip like this. With more conventional trips, like going into a campsite for several days, distances travelled are short and means for cooking are usually available once you get there. It's no big deal if you overstock. This was to be a no-frills trip, so we had to economize and keep the weight down. This was right up my alley.

Although we weren't planning to take in dry beans, molasses, oatmeal, and bacon, like our hero Titus Smith, we thought we should stick pretty darn close to his menu. We certainly weren't going to lug in tinned goods, like those poor guides had to in Albert Bigelow Paine's *The Tent Dwellers*. For sure, we weren't going to outfit ourselves like their "sports" did back in 1905. Those gents never had to carry more than a fishing rod, and, with their guides doing the work, their sojourn through Nova Scotia's woods was just a leisurely stroll. We wouldn't be following their example, even though we would be following their footsteps along part of the Shelburne River.

Doug and I counted on five days to get out and I translated that into a certain number of breakfasts, lunches, dinners, etc. Basically, we decided to do our own thing with respect to breakfasts. I went with oatmeal eaten out of a small saucepan, while Doug opted for the early morning air redolent with the aroma of frying ham or bacon.

Since Doug was to carry the tent, I agreed to supply the five evening meals (well, my wife did): three would be thick stews, and two, fish cakes of the special, homegrown variety. Lunch was corned beef—yep, in a tin—or peanut butter and bread; the firm, unsliced brown type, which packs well. Finally, there was the unavoidable snack food and the indispensable drink crystals.

Food naturally leads to pots, pans, and stoves. Sensible thinking was required in this department, but the mode of heating food took the most thought. Being true to my fixation for keeping it light and simple, I suggested we bring only one small stove but Doug said "Aw, what the heck," so two it was, one fuelled with iosol, the other with propane.

I was beginning to give serious thought to the weight of my backpack, which, according to the map, I would be carrying an awful lot of the time. So it was thumbs down for the usual lanterns. I would rig a candle lantern. I figured this would meet any nighttime requirement, but we threw in a couple of mini maglites as well.

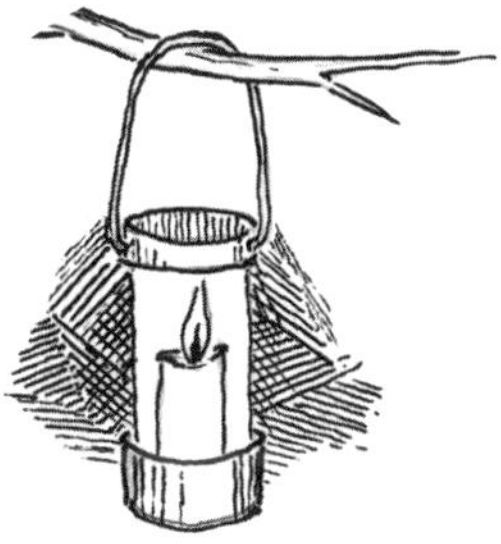

With all the little incidentals one is bound to throw in, I have found that having small, outside pockets on my backpack is a great way to store them—they're easy to get at without having to unship all the gear from your pack.

* * *

The main rule with clothing when travelling outdoors is to bring too much—too little puts you in a fine fix if it gets cold. I don't break that rule, even though it runs counter to my fixation. Even if you're travelling through the hottest part of the summer—which would not be advisable in the case of the Shelburne River because of low water levels—you should still be prepared for cold nights. You need to have a change of clothes as well. By change, I mean a set of long underwear, another shirt, and two extra pairs of socks. I brought one extra pair of socks.

For footwear, I opted for low rubber boots because mine were comfortable to walk in and would be easy to slip off once I was in the canoe—something I always do. But because I was afraid that putting insoles in my boots would make them too tight for quick removal, I didn't bring any along; a bad mistake I was to learn later.

Foot care is always an important piece of business with me during long trips through the woods, so I am embarrassed to admit to leaving my insoles at home. But I can now tell you that taking a five-day canoe trip, which requires as much walking as it does boating, and includes lining a canoe through long rapids, is, definitely, damned hard on the feet.

Still, you have to cut down on the amount of footwear you might normally take. Hiking boots come in handy, rubber boots are a necessity, and some sort of camp shoe would be nice, apart from the problem of weight and bulk.

Although Samuel Hearne probably had everything carried for him through the barrens, he suffered from the thousand-mile hike wearing only soft, non-weatherproof moccasins. There was no rubber footwear in Hearne's time, nor was there any in Titus Smith's in 1801, when he cruised through Nova Scotia assessing trees for the masts and spars of the Royal Navy. Smith walked for five months through the woods, and relates that he bored holes through the soles of his boots for reasons he didn't explain, but apparently it worked.

On a forty-eight-mile canoe trip with all the carrying involved, I figured I'd concern myself only with wet feet and camp comfort. It would have been nice to wear hiking boots while walking over hard and rocky ground, but I just couldn't afford the luxury.

We weighed our backpacks the night before departure. Doug's weighed fifty pounds and mine, forty-two. So my penchant for keeping it simple translated into eight pounds. Should I have scrimped to save so little? Time would tell.

Making the most of a short portage

You can't start a trip like this without the help of a good friend. We squeezed into Ivan's truck with all our gear, and the canoe lashed firmly in the back. We bounced along what is the last tentacles of man's encroachment into the province's last wilderness. It gnawed at us wondering if this encroachment would continue until the province's largest mainland moose herd is squeezed out of existence.

We began to get the feeling that we were actually getting away from it all. Cellular phones don't work in here! Oh for the glorious days of the 1970s when being in the woods was being in another world—like when E.R. Faribault camped on some moon bathed Nova Scotia lake with his survey equipment and the wild call of the loon echoing eerily through the night.

The last tentacle of civilization did peter out—right at the wreck of an old wood bridge that once spanned Hunting Lake Stream. Here we are!

Eager to get going on that warm and sunny afternoon in early May, we dumped our gear willy-nilly into the canoe, shoved off and, with a final wave to Ivan, headed upstream into the land of the moose.

Upstream we went, but we hardly noticed it because the stream was a flat meander north. The smooth water gurgled under my feet in the bow, and soon the constricted stream opened up to thirty yards bordered on both sides by a wide bog which finally gave way to scrubby black spruce and a low skyline. It was like something you'd see in the Northwest Territories. Giving life to the whole wild scene was the bird life—and it was bountiful. Red-winged blackbirds, grackles, and tree swallows (who were certainly the most curious of the lot), dipped and swooped around us, trying to figure out what we were. Black ducks and the flashy common mergansers avoided

us as they exploded from their nesting sites. Blue herons remained stately, but wary. The wildness around us was inspirational. Doug must have gotten carried away by it all, because he was sure he saw a Sissiboo Whip-poor-will.

With the soft and spongy shoreline all around us, it was surprising to look down through the tea-colored water and see a clean, gravelly bottom. Nothing was growing there. I've seen this before, and it always seemed strange to me until someone explained the phenomenon. These bogs contain sphagnum moss, which does not support any form of plant life, and its acid wastes build up as it decays, creating a sterile environment.

After a time of enjoying almost effortless paddling, we came upon our first rough water. We weren't sure what we were entering—was it a riffle, a rip, or a rapid? We watched it approach and knew it couldn't be a rapid, and it wasn't just a roughing of the surface, so we concluded it was a rip. It was a rocky run, but the hidden rocks were deep enough to allow us to pick our way smoothly, and we didn't hit one going through. Onto the flat water again, we flowed along in awe of the surroundings. The horizon off to either side was at about the same level as we were, so we felt we were amidst a great expanse of flat, primeval land. A contrail against the blue sky looked like it shouldn't be there.

Easy as our first little encounter with rocks was—hardly worth a second thought from experienced whitewater paddlers—it occurred to me that we weren't cruising a muddy meander through meadowland with nothing to do but look around; we had to keep our eyes down and sharp, and the paddle poised. Suddenly, the river constricted between fast encroaching spruce and pine trees to a point we knew we dare not enter. This was going to be our first carry.

The start of the carry was conveniently flagged by a little piece of red ribbon that surveyors use. Someone had intruded before us. What followed was a good lesson in how not to transport gear on a canoe trip. I feel a bit sheepish admitting we didn't exactly shine on our first portage.

We pulled the canoe onto a boggy spot and enthusiastically grabbed some gear—I a backpack and Doug the canoe—and off we trod along a barely discernible route through tight bog spruce, with a bit of ribbon every showing the way every once in a while. A very experienced canoer had given us a map with notations on it, and the notation for this carry said it would take five minutes with gear. Either memory failed him, or he was a super athlete, because it took us more than double his time.

We dumped our first load at the end of the carry, then went back for the remaining gear, only to discover we left too much for one carry. Doug took a pack and two paddles and I a bag and some loose stuff, but we had no free hands to carry what was left, including a third paddle. Pretty sloppy! So I had to return for the leftovers, which meant that I travelled the trail, although only half a kilometre long, five times. We felt pretty stupid, and were glad there was nobody there to witness it.

The first bivouac

The first lake we entered was more a surprise than anything else. It was really only a widening of the stream, but the map said Rush Lake, and that was as good a name as any. Bogs of sphagnum led to sedge grass, and finally black spruce, with spots of bulrush. Off to our right at the edge of a hillock we were surprised to see a burn spot. Several pine trees and sedge grass were scorched black. This natural burn, caused by lightning, complemented the wildness of the country we were entering.

We knew we were approaching our second carry somewhere not far ahead, so we blithely followed a lead through the bog, only to find we had been suckered into a dead-end and had to push ourselves backwards to where we could get turned around. "Over there by that nice pine knoll looks promising." And there it was, a landing spot for sure.

It would have been preferable, standing under widely spaced towering white and red pine, to have had this place absolutely pristine, but some nit-wit had left a sheet of cussed plastic draped over a jerry-built lean-to. We were glad, though, for a ring of rocks, some fire logs, and a soft bed of browned spruce boughs. It was now late afternoon, so we figured it would be a good idea to take the canoe and paddles to Sporting Lake, leaving us only one trip to make in the morning.

We had devised a shoulder pad arrangement on the thwart of the canoe that worked just great. And it's good it did because the notation on our map said this carry was fifteen minutes. It took us half an hour, spelling each other. We couldn't figure out why we were so off the mark because we didn't spare ourselves. So we consoled each other by agreeing that the notator had made a rough guess, on hindsight. The carry was one kilometre and, though not easy, was dry all the way. In places where the forest floor was clear, carpets of bunchberry bloomed, goldthread sprouted their three leaves up through moss, and the occasional painted trillium added a flashy bit of colour.

We rustled up the one indulgence we promised ourselves over an open fire—steak with onions and mushrooms. It's when you're sitting on a soft bed of pine needles, with your back against a tree, drinking tea and dodging the campfire smoke (which never fails to find you no matter which way the wind is blowing), that you speak of matters not connected with the work-a-day world; just lazy, carefree chatter where only time shows in light and shadow.

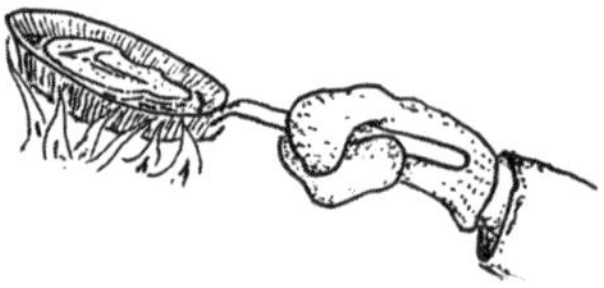

One mild concern were the bear claw scratches on some of the trees, so as a precaution we suspended our food between two trees, one of which a bear could easily have climbed and given the supporting rope a good swipe. We were in the tent by nine o'clock. We lit the candle lantern to build up some heat through the night, and no sooner had we wriggled ourselves comfortable into our sleeping bags than we were sawing wood.

No Picnic

Snug and warm like we were through the night, we were surprised when we picked up the teapot in the morning to discover the leftover tea frozen solid. Sun starting to poke through the trees, the campfire smoke hanging low in the still air, and the aroma of ham sizzling in the frying pan—it was enough to charm us into not wanting to leave. The aroma was Doug's contribution to the scene. With me, breakfast in the woods is more a pragmatic issue than a culinary treat. Get it over with, no fuss, and leave yourself the minimal amount of cleaning up. This meant dumping two packs of instant porridge into hot water in my small saucepan and eating it as is, scouring the pan and spoon by the water's edge with some moss, rinsing, and there you have it. All done! And not much character or colour to it either.

It was down to the canoe with one load each this time, and off we shoved onto Sporting Lake, the sun sparkling on the surface rippled by a westerly breeze. It was a restful paddle for a while, but as we got out onto more open water the ripples changed to waves slapping the side of the canoe, then to whitecaps. Suddenly we had one heck of a job on our hands. We wanted to go south but the wind said east, and it darn near got its way until, after about a mile, we got into the lee of land and gratefully made our way to shore.

On that hectic run, we had our backpacks tied to the thwart and our boots off. Crossing open waters in a stiff crosswind in a canoe is dangerous business and one to be avoided if possible. We could have followed a lee shore all the way, but on this lake that would have meant travelling an extra mile and a half. Better that than being dumped into the middle of the lake, I admit, but we did think we could make it straight across.

The land that now surrounded us was different from what

we had previously passed. The horizon was still low, but there was only hard shoreline now. This country is part of the Atlantic lowland, where granite and quartzite predominate, and the boulders strewn all over the lake were proof positive of that. It is no wonder that this country with its thin soils, rock, and poor drainage has remained wild. But it's great for the modern voyageur and the moose!

At the landing we wasted no time. One took the canoe and the other the two paddles. We had lashed the third paddle to the canoe, but it was just as easy for one of us to carry the other two paddles until it came his turn to take the canoe. Our map said this portage was twenty-five minutes with canoe, but we were onto that guy by now. We did it in forty, and were willing to bet that that was a pretty good effort. The one-and-a-third-kilometre stroll back took twenty-five minutes, but that's because we wanted to savour the landscape we had passed through, since we couldn't do that with our eyes fixed downward under our heavy loads.

A sixteen-foot seventy-five pound canoe is a good load for the average person. We've read of great feats of endurance by explorers and surveyors, but they never seem to record how long they walked before stopping for a rest. In the 150 days Titus Smith spent in the remotest hinterland of Nova Scotia, not once did he mention in his diary the weight of the load he carried. That would have been interesting to know, since he would have had to carry food and some form of shelter, and definitely an axe to construct the rafts he used to cross the rivers and lakes. What kind of condition was he in at age thirty-three almost two hundred years ago? Better than ours, I'd guess, although we've been told that men back then were shorter and weaker than men are today. This is difficult to accept from the stories I've read! But if we weren't a Titus Smith, were we a match for our map maker? I mulled this over as we plugged along, spelling each other before one got tuckered out, so on a one-kilometre carry, we would each have two turns at the canoe.

That wind from the west kept playing havoc with us along the upper section of Oakland Lake. The leeside we hugged wasn't much help because of the low horizon, but after a kilometre we entered a narrow waterway through a wide expanse of bog, then took a branch leading east away from the lake and headed to our fourth carry to East Cranberry Lake.

The map note said ten minutes with canoe. Boy, either we were lacking, or someone was doing some bloody awful bragging. This was just about the damnedest, most miserable route you could imagine, and only half a kilometre at that! Roots, rocks, windfalls, tight squeezes! There was hardly a place where you could aim the canoe straight ahead for even fifteen feet. Doug was lost ahead on my carry, scouting where next to go, when the exertion on my shoulders and arms just about did me in. In a momentary flash of total exasperation, I gave out one mighty yell for God knows whose benefit, but only the birds and animals heard me. Ten minutes? It took us thirty.

The handhold we added was made from a hockey stick screwed to the gunwales. Besides allowing us to direct the canoe through obstacles, holding onto it was restful for the arms. Gripping only the gunwales with your hands is okay for a short trip along a woods road, but is useless when making your way over rocks and through trees. Dipping the front under branches, lifting the tail to clear an obstacle behind, and directing, always directing, was a workout on the body I couldn't sustain for more than five minutes without a truce. Looking ahead at more of the same while your heart gradually slows down and you have a chance to wipe away the sweat from your eyes, was like facing an implacable enemy who would just not give way. It was only when you saw open space and some sky approaching that you realized that maybe you weren't going to die on the trail after all. As Doug remarked, "let me know when the fun starts, will you!"

* * *

The horizon surrounding East Cranberry Lake was even lower, which was understandable since the lake was at a higher elevation than where we had come from. This meant we were up against still stiffer winds. And rocks everywhere! Barren lands for sure! Except for the fact that it was completely pristine country, there wasn't anything nice about the surroundings; wild lands that not even the clear-cutters of today, let alone the loggers of yesteryear, cared to enter.

Time and deadlines are a curse on modern life. Everything has to be done by a certain time, otherwise your world will fall apart. We just can't help ourselves—the other fellow does it, so you do it too. And we were doing it here. The wearisome, thirty dips of the paddle per minute allowed no time for talk—just inner conversation with yourself. Sure, we had to fight the wind to get somewhere, but by now I was asking myself "what's the damn rush?" If the wind bothers you that much, just chuck the whole thing and go ashore and loaf around. I thought of Titus Smith. Sometimes he would stay put for a couple of days just doing nothing. You'll see me when I get there. But we dug deep with each stroke toward that six-day limit. It would have been nice to revert to "whenever."

How I wanted to linger at the start of our fifth carry leading to Clearwater Lake! It was picturesque. Clear ground beneath tall pines carpeted with needles and short grass, ideal for stretching out and resting the weary shoulders on a soft backrest, watching the sky go by through the boughs high above. The only unnatural thing in sight was a small circle of rocks with some old charcoal. So we left it as it was, and loaded up again, not wanting to add the least sign of our presence.

We sensed we weren't getting the full story when we checked the next notation on the map. It said twenty-five minutes with no gear. Now why would anyone say something like that when your only purpose back here was to carry gear? No gear! Good heavens, this was no Sunday stroll through the park. Doug and I had a good laugh thinking up explanations for that happy little entry. We finally decided that the only feasible answer was that the chap had a helicopter waiting for him while he took a stroll to the lake.

We took the packs first, in order to get an idea of what lay ahead. The first half of the route was through woods, and the remainder over hilly barrens, where we followed a moose trail. The moose droppings all along the way were the light-brown, pellet type, which suggested winter browse—kind of old. Although we tried to act like moose stalkers, there was no contest here, since those animals would know we were coming from far off. When I reflect on the fact that Titus Smith never once saw either a moose or a caribou through all his travels despite their many signs, we didn't feel so bad. And all the better! It's comforting to know our mainland woods can still harbour such a large beast in secrecy, where it can live unmolested. Just being in the primeval land would transform anyone from an indifferent bystander into a radical activist in the fight to keep what wildlands there are left—anywhere. Someone once said that when our wildlands disappear, so do we.

We often used the tumpline. Doug liked using it on all his carries, but I find it good going uphill only, when you can lean naturally into the weight. On the level or downhill, the tumpline tends to pull the head backwards, putting a strain on the neck muscles—that's what it does to me—but Doug liked it on all grades.

After thirty minutes we reached Clearwater Lake and more low horizon of black spruce in all directions, and rocks everywhere. Then it was back for the canoes, when our orderly routine of spelling each other broke down completely. Frustration with a litany of obstacles, and a lack of patience in facing them, did it. Windfalls in all the right places, and at the right height, can defeat you when you have to use one leg as a jack to get up and over them. We resorted both to carrying, then to dragging the canoe, and when we finally broke out of the tangle and the muck and emerged onto a barrens, we pushed and pulled through the foot-gripping sheep laurel, with the front man straining and the rear man stumbling and panting, until finally we ended a brutal hour by sitting at the water's edge and bathing our feet.

Driven onto a mean shore

One lake and one more carry, and tonight we'll be at the source of the Shelburne River—Buckshot Lake. The idea inspired us. Clearwater Lake is roundish and a kilometre in diameter, and it offered only open water, so the minute we shoved off we got smacked on our right side by the west wind which was stiffer than on our last encounter. Our boots were off, for sure! There were whitecaps more than a foot high, fighting to heave us over and our eyes were locked on the right with each frantic stroke of the paddle on our left. We weren't going south, we were being driven east, so not five minutes into our passage we obliged the wind and pointed towards shore, where we were sent with dispatch and no ceremony at all.

A moss and lichen garden this was. Brown Mane and Old Man's Beard clung to the branches, and lichens covered the trunks. The whole floor of soggy moss offered not one spot where you could set your rump in dry comfort. Picture in your mind an ideal campsite next to a lake where you could spend serene hours just doing nothing—well, this wasn't it. Instead, it was as miserable a spot as you could imagine.

Setting up camp while on the move for days in the woods becomes a ritual after a while. Each man lays out his things and claims his own space, generally marked by a tree or two. Camp etiquette says you don't use the other guy's tree. So Doug had his spindly black spruce and I had mine. Each tree held our clothes, and the mossy hump at its base was our work and storage area—two separate little kingdoms that lent good order to all the personal stuff strewn out on the least crummy spot we could find to pitch the tent. But we weren't so separate as to not heat up a delicious stew together, the aroma making our mouths water before it was even ready. I discovered I had lost my spoon, so with my knife, I fashioned a kind of spatula from a fallen limb, and it worked great.

Then each of us did his own woods scullery, my choice being wet roughage by the lake's edge, while Doug chose hot water and soap. A mealtime clean-up is almost enjoyable if done before a backdrop of those bucolic scenes you see on old calendars, showing a forked stick supporting a pot over a nicely arranged campfire, with men stretched out puffing on pipes—and maybe a string of trout between two trees—but for us it was just a menial place: no fire, no pipes, and no trout.

Someone said that doing this trip would be like going back into the nineteenth century. Well, it could have been the first century given the similarity of the landscape, but I know he meant being away from all the technology and modern cares. He was on the mark alright, since a cellular phone would be useless back here, and that definitely added to the mystique of this country as far as we were concerned.

With the mealtime chores done, and the inevitable smell of wet woolen socks being scorched over a burner adding some homeliness, we looked around for some natural history that might put some profit into idle time; but all we could accomplish was scraping some hard sap off a spruce tree and chewing it. The smooth-textured pink gum at least proved we were amidst black spruce and, with the barest of things to be done, we hit the hay and were out by nine-thirty.

Some map history

I'm going to leave the trail for a while in order to pass on some river-canoeing lore I got from an experienced canoer and kayaker who visited me to learn about our trip. I'll also comment on maps and mapping, specifically concerning the area we passed through.

River water conditions can be described as riffles, rips, and rapids. Riffles are moderately swift, shallow water, running over a gravel or sand bottom. Rips are swift-flowing deep water, running an irregular short course around exposed rocks. Rapids are swift-flowing water, tumbling with some force among obstructions, and are classified as one through six. (Canoe route maps for Nova Scotia are easily obtainable and give helpful descriptions for all six classes of rapids.) The rapids we encountered through the whole of our trip rarely got to class three, if that: rapids with high, irregular waves capable of swamping an open canoe with narrow passages that often require complex manoeuvring. I'd judge that the toughest we faced would be classed as a 2.5, since the waves couldn't be described as high, although they certainly were irregular, and some quick and tricky manoeuvring was required to prevent getting caught sideways. I know we didn't encounter class-four rapids, because they are described as generally not possible for open canoes—and should be attempted only by covered canoes and kayaks that are able to "Eskimo roll."

My visitor said he had had to "Eskimo roll" in Nova Scotia rivers, and that, fortunately, his head never hit rocks. Throughout our whole trip we never saw rapids where the water was that deep. Rocks lurking just below the surface were a constant menace where the bowman had to be quick to fend them off, or cue the sternman so he could react in time to steer the canoe clear. This type of bottom is referred to by experienced paddlers as "boney."

If one paddler is less experienced than the other, then surprisingly, the less experienced must take the stern where all he has to do is steer on cue from the experienced paddler in the bow. That paddler can spot danger, knows how to draw the bow one way or the other to avoid submerged rocks, and can react quickly in fending off rocks. His paddle work in drawing the bow to the right or left will cue the person in the rear to steer accordingly. Throughout our trip, I was the bowman, simply because I was lighter than Doug, which seemed to make sense, since we were not bow down. I don't know what an expert would advise if an experienced heavy-set paddler was working with a much lighter novice.

A haystack is an up-welling of water caused by a submerged obstruction. This formation reaches a sufficient height to spill over its edges, resembling a haystack. Nowhere did we see them that pronounced, but the ones we saw we took to be a sign of danger.

A "sweep" is another term canoers use. It is a tree fallen horizontally over the water with its broken limbs and boughs being swept by a fast current. Passing under these with sometimes no headroom—especially being driven down with no say in the matter—is a dangerous situation; you can get into trouble in the blink of an eye. We did come upon a few of those, but they didn't do any more than knock my hat off.

We were up on "lining," which was a good thing. We had a long line on each end of the canoe and one man would work them from his position upriver to point the canoe through obstacles—the other stationed himself down the bank to receive the boat and then a leap-frog exchange would be made. Through all these operations we felt confident enough to leave all the gear in the boat, which saved us an untold amount of labour. If the river had been in spate, however, we wouldn't have taken that chance.

On our trip, it became clear that deciding whether or not to run rapids has more to do with location than difficulty. Making a day run in a bathing suit and life-jacket, and carrying no gear makes tackling a class-four rapid mere fun, but in our situation, a rapid nearing a class three was scary. Being pitched into the water with your gear coursing out of sight was something you just can't allow to happen, since your life hangs in the balance, with hypothermia being the main enemy.

Getting through the rapids without being swamped and losing gear was a good example, in our case, of how the self-confidence of inexperience can sometimes work for you.

* * *

So you have a topographical map and you know where you are on the ground. The land and water you're passing through is shown, but have you ever wondered how the physical features got on the earlier maps, before aerial photography came into use in Nova Scotia in 1927? The quick answer is that most of them didn't and, if they did, they hardly resembled the actual thing. Many of the features, especially lakes, were either mislocated or misrepresented. Although damming altered the shape of many lakes and even created new ones, the physical impossibility of getting to every lake and stream in the province—together with the necessary surveying equipment, resulted in maps full of omissions and errors—and this up to as recently as the 1940s. The area of the province that most defied accurate mapping was the hinterland of southwestern Nova Scotia; in particular where the county lines of Digby, Yarmouth, Shelburne, and Queens converge. Here I get some real comfort knowing that the area is as it has always been and that I travelled through the past with all deprivations, except for maybe my iosol burner, nylon tent, rubber boots, etc.

I always wonder what earlier travellers had in the way of maps to guide them. Titus Smith is supposed to have carried a rough map of sorts; I bet it was rough! The only maps available in his time were lot and garden maps produced by the townships, which were mostly situated on the province's coast.

What aided Titus mostly, besides his compass, was a knowledge of the few roads that connected various settlements, like the one between Liverpool and Annapolis or Halifax and Windsor. He could always count on bisecting one of these eventually, in order to pick up provisions to last him and his assistant eight to twelve days. One day, on August 2, 1801, Titus decided to ration themselves to three biscuits a day, while they tried to procure game—he didn't say how—

but by August 8 they still hadn't gotten any, so they headed for the nearest settlement to get supplies.

The townships that were beginning to blossom around the province by the mid-eighteenth century were given some formal structure by the British governors. Each township consisted of one hundred thousand acres, under the authority of a township committee, which took over the responsibility for land division among the settlers and for the survey of lots. Thus began a piecemeal mapping of the province, which was to continue for the next two hundred years.

The Geological Survey of Canada began producing maps of 1/63, 360 scale (1 inch = 1 mile) in the 1880s. These maps also showed the waterways of the interior, with the expected errors and omissions, and they remained the most accurate maps available to woods travellers until the 1930s, when the Topographical Survey Bureau of the federal Department of Mines and Resources began issuing 1/63, 360 topographical maps based on aerial photographs. The 1/50,000 topographical maps familiar to us today began to appear about 1950. The earliest surveyors were often seamen using marine compasses, and only occasionally were these pioneer measurers properly trained in surveying. They took their base points from the nautical charts of the Nova Scotian coastline established by the Royal Navy, but once confronted by the dark forest beyond the garden plots of the townships, they probably saw no reason to continue going inland. They were stymied, anyway. The lack of proper surveying equipment plus facing what has been described as just about the most difficult and rugged terrain in North America, pretty well explains why our interior wasn't travelled by surveyors, and why our province has always been a draw to those who wanted to experience the mystical allure of the shadowy northern woods.

Now just to give you an example of how unreliable the maps in the 1920s were compared to modern-day maps, three maps are shown on the next two pages: one from 1924, one from 1954, and a present-day one, each of the same scale and each covering the exact same piece of the province. That there is practically no resemblance between the 1924 map and the other two, is not surprising, since mapping was such a hands-on business before aerial photography.

The Sissiboo Flowage, shown on the present-day map and to a lesser extent on the 1954 map, doesn't show on the 1924 map because it is a man-made reservoir. In 1927 the Digby County Power Board built a power plant at Sissiboo Falls, and through the late 1920s dams were built on lakes feeding into the Sissiboo, causing the backup of waters, which enveloped several lakes. Subsequent development has created what you see on modern maps.

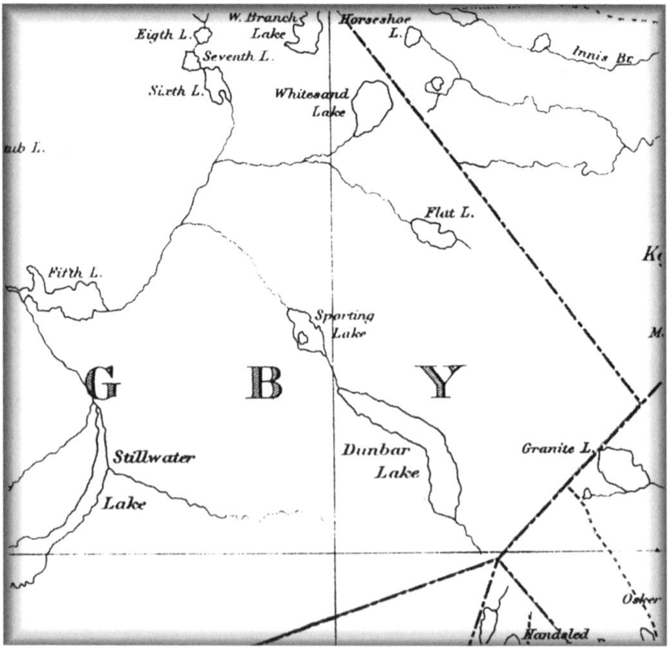

1924 Map.

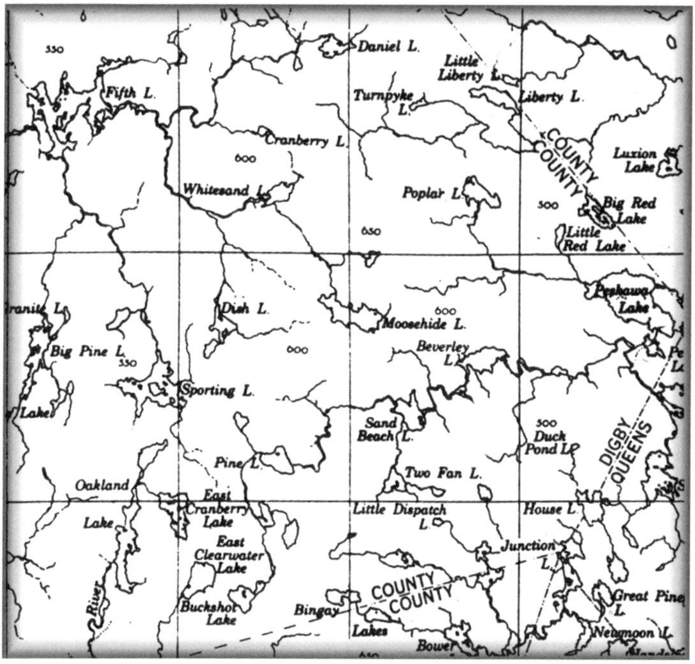

1954 Map.

Present-day Map.

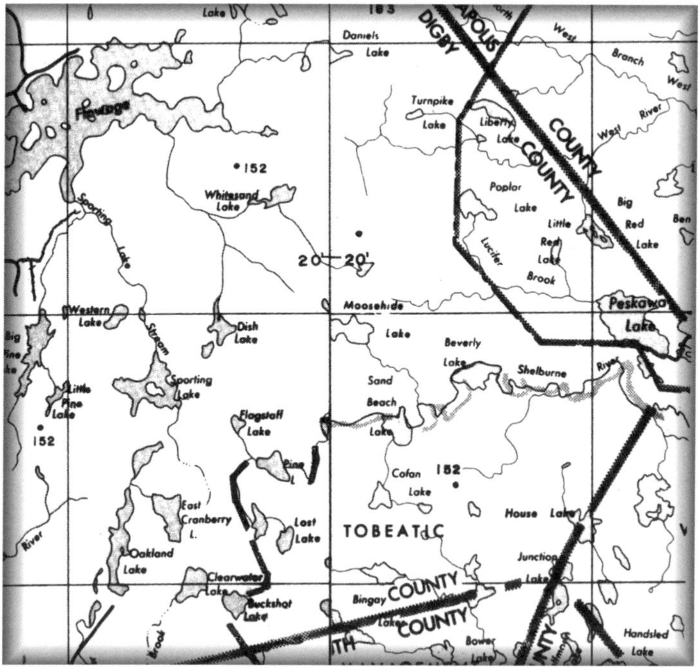

The source of the Shelburne

So it's back on the trail. Up at six o'clock; oatmeal and tea; patched boot where old patch came off; soles of my feet not in good shape—blanched from water, sweat, constant rubbing on hard sole; no insoles; we pack up; damn wind up through whole night, have to tackle it.

We couldn't just follow the half kilometre of shoreline to our sixth carry, but instead had to head out into the waves, then make a quick turn and run with the waves into the landing. And what do I find waiting there for me but a good pair of dry wool socks hanging from a limb of a pine. Thank you friend, whoever you are; I can sure use them.

This was a nice carry for a change, although, as usual, we didn't match the time noted on our map. It said 15-20 minutes with gear, while our backpacks took twenty minutes and the canoe forty. All carries necessitate that you travel the route three times, so we figured that was what the notator did as well.

The carry started off wet and through the shade of trees, then broke out into the open, and a dry, undulating barrens, spotted occasionally by small copses. The narrow foot-path through a mixture of stunted lambkill, low-bush blue-berry and teaberry still holding berries from the previous year, was obviously for the feet of moose. Their droppings all along the way were still disappointingly old. We tried to be quiet as we went, but those majestic creatures of these remote lands had long been spurred on by our clumsy entry into their territory. The herd here is as shy a group of animals as even seventeenth-century explorers found.

My first sight of the fabled Buckshot Lake—excuse the romanticizing—was from under the canoe, and it wasn't much to write home about. I saw only a wide expanse of lambkill which grabbed my boots at every step, and when I finally eased the bow down and got thankful relief for my shoulders, I saw only an unpicturesque setting, a barrens with low scrubby spruce and rocks, made inviting only by the fact that we had reached this milestone we had our hearts set on. Here was the source, the very beginning of the Shelburne River. For two men with lots of experience in the woods, this was still a thrill. We were like a couple of kids exploring something new and strange—we congratulated each other with a firm handshake, and gave out loud whoops of exhilaration.

The Shelburne River is unique in that it is wild from beginning to end. Isolated and difficult to access, especially the upper reaches, its very wildness led to its being declared a Canadian Heritage River in 1997.

Our map notator marked a spot on the south side of Buckshot Lake labelled "old sanctuary camp," so wanting to linger here and soak up the essence of the place, we went looking for the cabin. We couldn't find it, so we headed north-east to the river's head, the wind now favouring us for the first time and the weather sunny and warm.

Those experienced on this river say it should be attempted only in the spring and fall, when there is good water. The truth of their words hit home on the first two-kilometre stretch. Even in May, we still had to get out two or three times to ease the canoe around rocks, but mostly it was an easy paddle on flat water all the way, which meandered finally into Stoney Ditch Lake. If ever there was a granite rock garden, this was it! We entered the area called the Flintstone Granite Barrens, and the label says it all. The horizon all around is low and, although there's not a stick worth harvesting, the vast wildness is pure, raw beauty unthreatened by some road hidden behind the nearest trees.

You don't get to see much of Stoney Ditch Lake when you enter it, unless you take a detour from your passage. Our route hugged its western shoreline for only a short distance when we again entered the river and, for the next one and a half kilometres, it was easy going, happily cruising along flat, twisting water until the river began narrowing and then fell into enclosing forest. We got out to study the situation. It was here, also, that we got carried away by the self-confidence of inexperience. We failed to make a proper reconnaissance and decided, after a cursory look, to jump back into the canoe and head into this gloom that we knew nothing about.

Jim Charles

We might have gone a hundred yards at most. We should have realized a hundred yards was all we were going to get! We could have opted to portage, but we decided instead to unload and try to walk the canoe through—we'd load up again down a ways.

We didn't know that this section of the river was a carry. Doug was left with the canoe for three hours, while I had to investigate with the gear. We might have sighted each other twice through the whole struggle. Sometimes we were in voice contact or Doug would blow his whistle for me to answer with a yell, but our signals were mostly lost to the noise of the rushing water, and our minds were on our own jobs, trying to see some end to the damned situation we had stumbled into, while all the time wondering if we had gotten ourselves onto another track.

A confusion of divided water, side washes, fallen trees, and rocks! Doug had to do his work alone, since he had hip boots and, anyway, I had to worry the gear downstream, with the nagging thought that I wasn't really getting anywhere. My system was to take some gear along the most likely looking route—following the heaviest flow of water—return to get the second load, then explore ahead to determine where next to go. It was on one of these probes that I came upon two deer feeding; it must have been the noise of the rushing water that allowed me to get so close to them, but they quickly trotted off into dense cover.

We were feeling pretty stupid for having landed ourselves in this predicament, and I was soon to have this confirmed. Still groping ahead, I came to an unmistakable sign that I was nearing a lake—flat water opening into a stillwater. I was greatly relieved, and turned to rush back to tell Doug when I caught sight of a piece of faded red ribbon on a pine branch, then another one further away from the river. I had discovered the end of a carry!

Our trusty map of this section was faded, and we couldn't make out any sign of a carry, but there was one mark we could distinguish: a sanctuary cabin that was unusable. I followed the clear trail back and found it. Unusable alright! All that remained was a rusty set of iron bunks standing gauntly in a lumpy bed of moss. Now it was back to Doug, where we took the canoe out of the tangle—counting that struggle as our seventh carry—and got it to open water.

Pine Lake was another rock garden, but its flinty countenance was softened by beautiful, large, pure stands of tall pines. You could tell this part of the province got a good scouring from the ice cap—outcrops of bedrock, thin soils, and eskers—the gravelly residue left by streams and rivers flowing under the melting ice. These straight, elevated ridges topped along their length with white pine were now becoming prominent. As we made our way east across the lake we could see a long one to the north above the bog and scrub spruce.

It was a good paddle with the still-brisk west wind helping us along, until we saw the telltale sign of a pocket of maple and alders, which signals the start of a stream leaving a lake. This was going to be our spot for the night. Looking above at the towering pines, we expected to find firm and open ground where we could make a comfortable bed but, instead, the whole floor was nothing but mossy hummocks with practically no place to spread out a sleeping bag. Well, you take what you can get once you accept that the ideal campsite existed only in a painting. We put the tent up anyway, and had our choice of headrests and handy bumps.

My nicely packed and frozen fish cakes were now mush, and if I ever make a trip like this again, that's just the way I'll pack them (I don't know why I didn't do that in the first place). We made ourselves a good meal of this hash and weren't the least bothered it wasn't in its traditional shape. Of all the little chores we busied ourselves with here, the best for me was cutting down to size an extra pair of felt insoles Doug had found in his pack, and the relief to my woebegone feet was as sweet as you could want. Ah, the feeling! So, bushed like we were, we slept like babies even if we had to contort our bodies to fit the lumps, and when we got up at six o'clock we were fresh and eager to get going, which wasn't surprising since there was nothing beguiling enough about this place to keep you there.

The significant Sand Beach Lake lay ahead, eight kilometres downstream along which we had to make two carries of about three quarters of a kilometre each. Our campsite was the start of the first carry, our eighth, and when we put in again, we passed through class-one rapids, then class-two, until we came to class-three waters, which we weren't going to deal with, so we carried again, our ninth—a tiring, sweaty one through woods then barrens in hot, sunny weather. When we got back into the canoe for the final run to Sand Beach Lake, we were in the mood to have as easy time of it, and that we got. This was easily the best run we had so far, noiselessly flowing along a wide, lazy route bordered by a broad expanse of bog, where the tall lines of pine and a cloudless, brilliant blue sky were perfectly mirrored in smooth water. The whole picture couldn't have been better retouched than with the largest mayfly hatch I have ever witnessed.

We had to stop along the edge of the bog just to watch this springtime phenomenon, the dancing clouds of gossamer wings shimmering in the sunlight—nature's own sparkling fireworks. With all the spent bodies littered over the surface of the water, you'd expect to see trout enjoying their favourite food, but there wasn't one slurp. Maybe the fish were glutted. The first casualty from acid rain on a fresh waterway is the mayfly, so this hatch indicated that this part of the province isn't as badly affected by acid rain as we supposed, I sure hope. Although we had a spinning rod, we didn't once try for trout, simply because of the challenges we were up against from dawn to dusk.

The flat, placid water took a wide sweep to the left, and on the right of our gentle entry to Sand Beach Lake was a long esker crowned with pines. Our map noted that this formation was once the hideout of Jim Charles. Another note indicated the location of a usable sanctuary cabin. I'm anxious to get to that cozy old log cabin, but first I have to explain about Jim Charles, whose life and memory are as much a part of this area as are the silent pines.

* * *

Jim Charles was a Mi'kmaq who was born around 1830 somewhere in the forests of western Nova Scotia. A document shows he purchased one hundred acres on Kejimkujik Lake in 1862 from one John Jeremy for sixty dollars. There, he and his wife, Lizzie, kept some cattle and made butter, which was regularly shipped to Annapolis Royal by mail coach. One spring in the early 1870s, Jim Charles divulged to his friend, Judge Ritchie of Annapolis Royal, who often came to Kejimkujik to fish with Charles, that he had discovered "brown silver." The judge determined it was gold alright, and for the next few years took delivery of Jim's gold, sent to him hidden in Lizzie's butter tubs, and arranged the sale of it through a bank in New England. Some of the proceeds he'd take to Jim, but he banked most of it in Jim's name in a bank at Annapolis.

Eventually, Jim Charles hankered for more spending money, and began travelling to Annapolis to withdraw it and make purchases there, then to Halifax, where he found the shops full of mouth-watering items, from the finest rifles and shotguns to saddlery and carriages and finery for Lizzie. By now, Jim and Lizzie were a spectacle, and there were those who watched Jim's every move, hoping to discover the location of his mine. One such character was a white man named Hamilton, who lived nearby with a Mi'kmaq girl. One day, Hamilton, full of rum, brazened himself into Jim's cabin demanding to know where the gold was. A fight ensued and, when Hamilton knocked Lizzie to the floor, Jim grabbed one of his guns and gave a mighty smack to Hamilton's head with the butt, killing him.

A shopkeeper named Harlow, who acted as the local magistrate, lived fifteen miles away in Caledonia and it was to him that Jim ran in a frenzy with his team of horses to explain what he had done. Harlow heard him out, then quickly assembled a coroner's jury, and away they went to Jim's cabin on Kejimkujik to examine the corpse and take testimony from Lizzie and Madeleine, Jim's adopted daughter. The verdict of the inquiry was "death by misadventure," which just about everyone agreed with, saying Hamilton got what he deserved. But there were others who thought Jim a murderer who should be hanged.

Nervous about the feelings some of the white locals held against him, and unsure just how far the coroner's verdict would protect him, Jim decided not to take a chance, so with his birchbark canoe, some supplies, a gun and ammunition, he took to the woods. Thomas Raddall in his story *The Lost Gold at Kejimkujik* gives the most authoritative account of the saga of Jim Charles. The source of much of what he reported came from the Reverend Clayton Munro, who grew up in Caledonia and who knew Jim Charles. Reverend Munro died in 1950 at the age of eighty-six, so his time easily overlapped that of Jim's, who died in 1905.

Jim went to the south end of Kejimkujik Lake, then made the several portages familiar to present-day canoers, to arrive on the Shelburne River. He proceeded upriver, or westward, going ever deeper into the land of mystery, known only to himself and the occasional lone trapper. This would have been in the late 1870s. Raddall was able to establish that Jim turned off the river to a small lake lying just to the south of it, called Couffin Lake. It is this bit of information that perplexes, which I'll explain later, when I get to the old sanctuary cabin Doug and I were anxious to reach.

It seems an Acadian trapper in much earlier days named the lake Couffin, a French word for a basket made of rushes or wood splits. Whatever the reason for the Frenchman giving it that name, the Mi'kmaq also used it, except that it came out as "koofang" in their pronunciation. On maps produced in the 1920s the lake doesn't even show; it does show on a map for 1954, but is called Two Fan. A mispronunciation of "koofang" I would guess. On modern maps it now shows as Cofan Lake (see map on p.25). If you compare old maps with new, you'll find many examples of name changes, omissions and wrong locations. With that aside, I'll take you briefly through Jim Charles' remaining days.

Three years after his disappearance, Jim reappeared to take up his usual life at his cabin with Lizzie and Madeleine. As far as anyone knew, he had not been seen during that time, although some suspected that Lizzie and Madeleine travelled by canoe to his hideout to take him supplies.

Lizzie died not long after and Jim took up homemaking with Madeleine, who bore him a son, who, when grown-up, went to the United States, and never came back. People still wondered about Jim's "Eldorado," but he never got gold from his secret spot again and here's why. One day not long after his return, he headed out with a woodsman friend, hoping to "stake" his claim and then register it with the Department of Mines. Jim and his friend reached what is now called Buckshot Lake, portaged—as near as can be figured—to Clearwater Lake, and then to Oakland Lake, the source of the Tusket River. Somewhere near the beginning of the Tusket River they came upon a stamp mill in full activity. Someone had discovered Jim's "mother lode," and was busily mining it, so there was nothing left for him to do but go home empty-handed. The trip proved that Jim's gold didn't come from around Kejimkujik, as everyone suspected, but much further west in country no one ever imagined.

Jim Charles' last years were bereft of good health and dignity. Severely crippled with arthritis, and mentally ill as well, he died in the care of a Mi'kmaq family near the village of Milton, around 1905. He is buried in an unmarked grave near Saint Gregory's Church in Liverpool.

* * *

After photographing Jim Charles' supposed hideout, we took the wide sweep into Sand Beach Lake, and were confronted with a body of water studded with granite boulders. Threading our way through the granite, we turned a point and were presented with a beautiful little sandy beach. The moment we stepped onto the fine, cream-coloured sand, we felt like intruders, for there were the imprints both of moose and of deer. The beach was small, not more than fifty feet long, and shelved down gradually, the water fading from a tea colour to the deep blue of the reflected sky. Across the still waters we could see two other beaches gleaming brightly in the hot sun, inviting to visit, but since we had our minds set on reaching the log cabin, we pressed on.

Reaching the east side of the lake, we entered the river again, which now was really a long stillwater turning abruptly to the north. There was the refuge we were longing to reach. I would have expected a better siting for the cabin, fronted as it was by low bog, which, though fairly dry now, would surely be under water during a spring run-off. The cabin was set on a piece of slightly higher, firm ground in a grove of tall white pine. For once, we would be able to relax, and not have to bother with setting up and taking down, while also having a hot stove to enjoy.

The cabin is built of pine logs, and measures fifteen feet, ten inches wide, by nineteen feet, eight inches long. The name carved on the board befuddled me. What looks like a skull beside the window is actually the pelvis of a young white-tailed deer. There are asphalt shingles on the roof. Some of the side logs are butted, not being long enough for the required length. There is a window on the far and rear walls.

Inside, there is a box of firewood on either side of the door. An iron wood stove to the right is of the style you often find in old woods cabins—the top heating surface flared out in front to hold two larger plates—made by The New Burrell-Johnson Iron Co. Ltd. of Yarmouth. Against each side wall is a set of iron bunks with springs but no mattresses, just planks.

A table with two benches, pots and pans, a cupboard, a shelf across the back wall holding condiments, and the ever-present camp log, completed the very cozy interior. I haven't found anyone who knows when the cabin was built, but I would guess it was in the 1940s.

We got a fire going, not because we needed the heat, just for the cheeriness a wood stove gives. We did our much-needed laundering and hung it by the stove to dry. It says something about this life when you get real pleasure out of doing something as menial as washing. We lazed around, took photographs then cooked up a good meal of fish mush and strong coffee.

Later on, with a couple of candles flickering, and a deer mouse scampering around in the shadows, we read the log and recorded our visit. The log dated back only to 1990, and some of the parties on record had visited more than once. Some of these folks started at Lake Joli, which is southeast of Bear River;

a greater distance than from where we started—but it appeared they doubled back the way they came, without continuing along the Shelburne to Lake Rossignol.

One note, which I took for gospel at the time, said that Sand Beach Lake used to be called Cofan Lake, explaining the name on the front of the cabin. Thomas Raddall's research doesn't support this; neither does my own subsequent research with old maps. What was the reason the builders named the cabin Cofan? Perhaps Raddall's informant was a bit foggy on this account.

A.F. Church, who produced maps of the province through the latter half of the nineteenth century, shows blank spaces where Sand Beach and Cofan Lakes should be, and for that whole section of the province for that matter. E.R. Faribault and Hugh Fletcher, two of those late nineteenth-century hardy surveyors for the Geographical Survey of Canada in Nova Scotia, were unfortunately never able to survey the south-western part of the province and produce reasonably accurate maps like they did for the rest of the province.

It would be nice to sit with someone who had a hand in building the cabin on Sand Beach Lake, but most likely none of them are still alive. It is a fact, however, that the guides from the Bear River area always refer to Sand Beach Lake as "koofang," and whether or not this was based on some false assumption we'll never know. I might eventually get to solve the puzzle of Couffin (Two Fan or Cofan?) Lake and where Jim Charles' hideout really was, but there's an allure to mystery, so perhaps I'll leave it alone.

There is another example of how mapping of this area differed through the years. The three maps on pages 24-25 cover the same piece of territory. Dunbar Lake, shown on the 1924 map, is a mystery to me; you can see that it never existed. The map doesn't have the slightest resemblance to the other two, which, of course, are based on aerial photographs. The 1954 map shows Two Fan Lake (Couffin?) just to the south of Sand Beach Lake. The present-day map shows Cofan Lake.

One last example of how far off the mark that 1924 map

is: Granite Lake appears to be the source of the Shelburne River. Where are the other forty kilometres of river continuing westward? What's harder to understand is that in *The Tent Dwellers*, published in 1908, Albert Bigelow Paine calls it Irving Lake—as indeed it was known then, as it is today.

The weather changes—as do our fortunes

It wasn't easy saying goodbye to Cofan Cabin, and the comfort it provided, so we took our time leaving, shoving off at eight o'clock. I often feel sympathy for woods cabins like this. They live a life of prolonged periods of utter loneliness through sun, rain, and blizzard, interspersed with the briefest periods of companionship that they can't really enjoy because they know they'll soon be abandoned again. When I turned around to take one last look at good ol' Cofan, I felt a twinge of regret, knowing that this would probably be the last I'd ever see of it.

We made an abrupt turn to the north along a stillwater through wide bogs, and came upon a scene out of an old print: a moose lifting its head out of the water, holding a mouthful of dripping plants. But they had gotten wind of us—again. It was still sunny and warm as we went along, sometimes with the wind at our backs, sometimes with it hitting us broadside as we followed the turns. The wide river's course took us through a landscape ground flat by glaciers, with isolated stands of trees and bushes giving contrast to the monotony of it all, until we found ourselves entering Beverley Lake, which could be mistaken for another widening of the river where it had flooded a boulder-strewn depression.

This was a lake that you just wanted to get across, because nothing interesting caught your eye unless you were a geologist or a botanist studying peat bogs, and even then I don't think they would have had much fun doing it. We set our eyes on the east end of the lake two kilometres away, where the river started again, and kept our minds on a notation on our map that cautioned against wind and rocks—that fellow wasn't fooling—when finally we approached a different landscape. Here was a boreal forest again showing the mysterious dark depths that put the glint in your eye, wondering what you are being taken into.

As we nosed in closer, we could see there was a choice to be made. With paddles athwart, and the canoe slowing losing its momentum on calm water, a deep defile presented the outflow—a narrow, tumbly looking exit with windfalls laying across it. Maybe if we were more experienced, and wearing light clothes with no kit, we would have tackled it, but a quick look at the map showed "rough, class three," so we decided to back off. Besides the map indicated another way to get there. We backtracked and rounded a point into a narrow, deeply wooded cove that ended in a point, and a piece of red ribbon. That was for us, alright! Our tenth carry!

The disappointing thing about carries is that you don't often get to see the rapids and scenery you are bypassing. This one, only about 350 metres through open woods, was an easy carry; we strolled along with nothing much to see but darn glad to be without the muscle-straining ducking and twisting when even your backpack snags on something, and you have to constantly ward against having an eyeball rasped by a spiny spruce branchlet. The memory of being blinded in one eye for a day by one of them made me appreciate this carry that much more. There are lots of stories of people who have suffered serious eye damage from pokes in the eye; one man I know was blinded in one eye for six months by such an encounter. Travelling as we were beyond any help, the spectre of one of us becoming maimed still gave only the briefest shudder before it slipped from mind, because we were passing through an absolute wildness that seemed to embrace and protect us.

We came out to a beautiful stillwater where we had to stop to take it all in, munching on corned beef sandwiches and dipping a cup of the cool water from the constricted river rushing in over rocks and gravel. What a place to cast out a line into the foam and bubbles for a sure strike, but our one little spinning rod was at the bottom of the pack, and the inviting water insisted that we see it now—our life was still being directed by that damned thing: time.

On the Shelburne River, which begins at Buckshot Lake and runs for fifty-three kilometres, passing through seven more lakes until it empties into Lake Rossignol, you get plenty of changes in water types, and sometimes they come with little warning. It's enough to keep you keyed up to make the right move when its needed—you hope. We were still the runners of the woods, probers of the deep, lulled into a reverie by the pleasantness of it all, when all of a sudden we were met by rapids (class two the map said), but there was no hesitation, and in we went and great fun it was, too. We picked the right spots, running between rocks, sidestepping others, and breathing a near-audible sigh of relief when we finally raced out onto flat water, and smoothly picked up with a rhythm of strokes to match the speed we had been driven into. What exhilaration that was for two unpractised rapid runners like us, luckily meeting that extra dash of danger this country with its dark frown can throw at you for the least lapse of attention to it! But we weren't so overconfident as to think we could beat this thing just yet.

* * *

We glided out onto Granite Lake, commenting that the map makers back then didn't need much imagination to come up with the name. We got across to the east end quickly, where we had to choose between making a carry or running class-two rapids, so we chose the rapids, which ran for perhaps 250 metres. We had a busy time of it, but there was a good flow of water that easily sent us racing down river, where we again ran out onto flat water for the next kilometre and a half until we came to the start of the Granite Falls. No choice here but to make another carry—our eleventh.

With our heads bent down from the tumpline or stuck inside the canoe, we didn't get to see much of this kilometre of tumbling, heaving waters; the mere glimpse we had at the start was soon lost. But the forebearers of Jim Charles must have made this ancient trail to bypass the impassable stretch of water so we knew we were in good company as we struggled along its desolate and solitary route. The carry took twenty minutes for the gear and forty with the canoe, but it was a nice one, descending all the way along a smooth path through an open mixture of spruce and hardwood and, according to our trusty map, it would be our last one, too. This was going to be a cinch.

We came out to Pebbleloggitch Stillwater and the historic crossroad, you might say, for all those who ever travelled the river by way of Kejimkujik Lake. Here you decided either to head west and upriver, or to turn southeast and down river to Irving Lake and eventually to Lake Rossignol. This was the crossover point Jim Charles always used, and as we paddled along its smooth waters, I could see to our left the exact exit point he made from Pebbleloggitch Lake. Here is another example of just how incompletely mapped this area was, as recently as the 1920s: the two sports in *The Tent Dwellers* who came out at this same exit point thought, or so their two guides told them, that they were now on the upper Shelburne River as they headed east to Irving Lake, a stretch we now know as the lower Shelburne. In other words, they figured they had come out at the start of the river.

Once across the stillwater we entered the river proper again; two and one-half kilometres of sometimes winding, sometimes straight, flat water with forest sometimes close in, then giving way to wide bog margins. We finally coasted into Irving Lake, the largest of all we had passed through, spiked with much granite despite the fact we were now in a gentler land. This name of this lake is just one of many examples throughout the province of how mapmakers and surveyors often either didn't ask the locals or didn't consult earlier maps; the 1924 map calls this Granite Lake, while in 1908, *The Tent Dwellers* calls it Irving Lake. I wonder what earlier travellers called the Granite Lake we passed through upriver—although they would never have found it on a map then.

The names Beverley, Pebbleloggitch, and Irving came from

persons now lost in the mist of time, although the second is by far the most original. All the eight lakes that garland the Shelburne River probably had native names before the French settlers began probing its mysteries, but the ones they coined have mostly stuck down to the present.

So we beat across Irving Lake with rain now starting, although it was warm enough, and took a cautious look at where it emptied out into river again. We guessed we were entering class-two rapids; they looked tame enough, so we entered. At this point we realized we were on our own, since our map with all its helpful notations had suddenly stopped telling us anything, because it had been made for canoers leaving Pebbleloggitch Stillwater and traversing up into Kejimkujik Lake—not for those, like us, continuing on to Lake Rossignol.

Many people have accessed this river from Kejimkujik Lake and gone down to Lake Rossignol, including those sports in *The Tent Dwellers*, and they all say the same thing— this part of the river is just one tough son-of-a-gun of a stretch. Someone could have told Doug and me that there was a land route available to get down river, but we didn't know that at the time, so in we went.

For probably three hours in the drizzle, along a river not much more than thirty metres wide, with dripping forest overhanging, we ran waters, alternately fraught with danger of being caught sideways and being dumped, or struggling around sidewashes and blowdowns with the canoe lined down. Patience gets you through, just so long as you watch your step and don't make a stupid stumble, putting the other guy in a position where he has to somehow make good what you fouled up. So far, things were going pretty well for us. When we saw some good water we'd jump in and have a thrilling ride fending off fast-approaching boulders, or we'd grab for the shore just in time before hurtling into bad-looking stuff and line again. The thought crossed my mind that back ninety years ago those two sports in *The Tent Dwellers* chose to walk this same stretch of river with their fishing rods, leaving their two guides to wrestle the two canoes and all the gear down these rapids for most of a day, without having any idea, or concern for that matter, how they were making out.

Our exhilaration got the wind knocked out of it on one of our turns in the canoe. We suddenly got turned sideways against a rock just before a sudden drop, the onrushing water slamming against us until we could feel the canoe about to yield to the overwhelming pressure, and us desperately trying to prop it up with our paddles. We held it, and realized we could step onto a rock, enabling us to get the canoe turned in line with the flow, but there was only room for one of us on the rock, which meant I was going to have to get to shore. I got there, mostly wet, and with a badly bleeding thumb, which got jammed between my paddle and a rock on one of my stumbles, and was finally able to receive the canoe Doug sent down to me on the long tether.

One more hour of struggling around fallen trees and rocks that were in all the wrong places used up all the patience we had stored up, although finding a good aluminum paddle and a boot along the way made us thankful we hadn't met the same misfortune. We quit at seven to make camp.

Sudden changes in geology

To make camp? What a euphemism that was, driven as we were into the soggiest, most God-forsaken spot on the face of the Shelburne. It was pure desperation that did it. There was no room to pitch our small tent, so we had to cut down three trees to make room. Then we stashed our gear under the overturned canoe. That was the easy part; the tough part was getting the sleeping bags arranged inside the tent, getting out of our wet clothes, and preparing something hot to eat and drink while crouching on the soggy moss with the rain running up noodles put a better cast on things when we were finally able to wriggle into our sleeping bags.

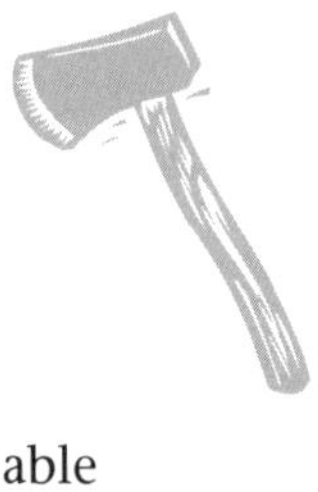

It wasn't so much the puddle you found leaking into your

sleeping bag at a spot you could hardly avoid, or the wet jacket you had for a pillow, or the fact that you were damn uncomfortable that gave you the miseries—it was the dripping on the tent, and the constant roar of the rushing river right beside you that told you you were going to wake up to face more of the same in the morning. The candle lantern would have given some heat inside the tent, except that one of Doug's motions while trying to get arranged knocked the thing flying, spilling hot wax everywhere, so that was that—the hell with it. A tired body will give way to sleep even in the most miserable of conditions, and that it did, and when we woke at six o'clock we didn't want to leave our bags—the part that was dry, that is.

It was back into wet clothes, and the rain still dripping through the soggy spruce didn't cheer us any. There was one little episode, though, which gave us a good laugh and put us into a good humour, which was just the medicine we needed to face the dreary scene: Doug preferred his propane burner to my naphtha stove, priding how quickly it lit and heated, but when he went to light his stove to heat our thick stew, he discovered that he hadn't shut off the valve the night before, so his tank was empty. Well, I didn't crow too little as I pumped up my stove and heated up the stew and tea in no time.

We got out of that place as quickly as possible, trying to build up some heat inside our wet clothes, and continued lining towards canoeable waters, which were about half a kilometre away. By now we were fed up with this lining business. We'd sooner carry any time. There was no nice clean bank along this river, only overhanging obstacles and flooded places, and when we'd get to a dangerous-looking section, we'd remove the backpacks before bringing the canoe down. This is when I appreciated what Titus Smith went through when he reported that he had to quit travelling whenever it rained heavily, because it soaked his pack, making it too heavy to carry—just like my vintage canvas backpack was beginning to feel.

Whatever might have been nice to look at and enjoy was lost to us in our more than four hours of scrimmaging with this infamous section of the Shelburne, and what made it all the worse further along, was seeing a ridge with open woods along the opposite side—perfect country for carrying, but it was in accessible, and remained a reminder of how not-too-smart we were.

Ever since we entered this section of river at Irving Lake, all of the granite we had seen before was no longer evident; I could tell because the rocks I was now stepping on were slippery—you had to watch every step, and that was probably my main beef about lining here. This stuff was nicely polished slate and greywacke, and made me slip and go over my boots so often that I stopped worrying about it, just so long as we were getting through this demonstration on how to line, which we could have done without.

After a while we broke out of this litany of bad waters, and the canopy of dripping forest, and shoved out onto wide, slow river where even the rain didn't bother us anymore. Things seemed to come alive after our seclusion in the shadowy gloom with ducks paddling quietly into their hidden nesting spots, a turtle watching from his rock perch, and muskrats slipping beneath the surface after getting a look at us.

Now we were on the lower Shelburne, where it swept lazily around bends with some narrow bog margin, and hardwood just starting to turn green. Every once in a while we would meet rapids, but they were only short ones of about fifty yards, adding just the right amount of spice to liven things up—each time we got ferried out onto flat water by a strong, boiling current, we felt its momentum sending us to our destination.

Going around a gentle bend in the river at about noontime on our sixth day, we were surprised to see a wooded bridge ahead. Here was the entry into Sand Lake, the last in the garland of the Shelburne. The rain had stopped for now, but the sky threatened more with the southeast wind keeping it heavily overcast. Here we stopped, and for me it was relief to take off my boots and wring out my socks and my pant legs. From here it was six miles to the mouth of the Shelburne, but it was the six-mile passage across the top of

Lake Rossignol that was on our mind, because this determined where we should make the next camp.

After two days of being in wet clothes, except when I was in my sleeping bag, which also wasn't all that dry, I was chilled to my innards, and the only way I could stop shivering was to keep moving, so I walked the road for half an hour, but the good effect was only temporary—you either move constantly or you get dry and warm somehow. When I returned, we decided the best thing was to get back in the canoe and cover as much of the river as possible before making camp—and be placed just right to tackle the final leg of our journey the next day.

Rain again, with the promise of more to come! So we were a soggy looking spectacle, but it was hard to dampen our spirits because we knew we were going to reach the mouth of the Shelburne. Buoyed up by this prospect, we sailed along fully confident of entering the river again two miles down, but after a while, it was clear we didn't know exactly where we were. Sand Lake is broken up with islands and deep coves, which appear to lead somewhere, but don't. We'd take one route, only to find a dead end or pass up another one. Then we turned into what we thought was the last section of lake leading to the river, quickened our strokes, rounded another point, saw a bridge far ahead, and made for it.

Talk about a damper! How did we ever manage this? After an hour of paddling we ended up right back where we started! Well, it was back down the lake again for another try, but that old confidence was starting to falter, so we decided to land and get out the map. In the shelter from the rain under a stand of large pines, we couldn't seem to match the map with the actual ground, but when you're shivering and hungry you easily lose the concentration needed for even simple mental tasks, and this was one of those times, so the decision was made. We'd quit and make a decent camp right here "mid the pines," then be rejuvenated to make the finish the next day.

To Rossignol

Tent up on firm ground, a large sheet of plastic draped over a rope strung between two trees providing a dry place to work, and it was looking pretty cosy, but we needed heat. It's one thing to get a fire going in wet woods, but when there's no spruce around to supply those always reliable starter branchlets, the job is going to take a lot longer, especially when you're working with wet pine. I could see that the forest across this narrow section of the lake was mostly spruce and fir with a fringe of birch and maple bordering a bog further along the shore and, since I could only stop shivering when I was moving, I decided that what I needed was work, so I paddled across to it.

Doug had things ship shape when I returned with the canoe full of spruce branches and birchbark and, with the oil of wintergreen igniting even though the bark was wet, we soon had a good fire going under our polyethylene shelter. Now I was able to remove my rain gear to get rid of the dampness trapped inside, and to relax for a change, washing down corned beef sandwiches with hot noodle soup, and building a contraption for hanging wet clothing by the fire. My gosh, we were having fun again!

One item of camping gear that is a necessity on lengthy trips like this, especially in the early spring, is a dry bag for holding extra underclothing, and Doug's came in handy now. Naturally, I didn't have one, given my penchant for travelling light and simple, but did I feel good when I put on his extra sweatshirt and longjohns and got into my sleeping bag!

This was almost as enjoyable as Cofan cabin. Looking out through the open tent flaps, my eyes were transfixed by the dancing flames. Doug had himself nicely supported with a comfortable headrest close to the fire, looking just like an old calender scene and, as it got darker, the shadows from the flames seemed to magnify on the inside wall of the tent, putting a cheery light on the whole surroundings, even though it was still raining. Then fast asleep at nine o'clock.

The polyethylene canopy sure added comfort when getting going at six o'clock, keeping the drip from the trees off us, and letting us prepare a good breakfast in an unhurried state. By the time we got everything packed it was after seven, an hour later than we would've liked.

We were anxious to see where the river continued again and where we went wrong the day before, so we followed the same route, rounded a point as before, but instead of continuing around we nosed into a cove we had earlier passed up, and were surprised to see that it opened up and went southeast. It was definitely the outlet. In our haste the day before, we had completely circled a long island, which we had taken to be a narrow peninsula.

The river literally sneaks out of Sand Lake at a spot that fooled us. It exits through a narrow shallows hidden mostly by clumps of meadow grass and flows two tight channels over beds of sand, then widens into a beautiful, long stillwater with its banks wooded to the edge with pine and hardwood just taking on a soft yellow-green tinge of colour. This was country that beckons you to slow down and admire it, for this is the soft and gentle Shelburne meant to charm the wayfarer as a reward for having endured the hard demands of the flintstone land.

The stillwater suddenly got pinched between two points of stately pines, where a slight downgrade makes the water race fast and deep—a fly fisherman's dream of a spot—before it flows out into more of a long lake than an actual river. It was as we were passing down its middle that we saw two deer give us a flash of their white flags before disappearing into the forest.

It wasn't long on this passage before we were once again interrupted in our reverie of being beyond the doings of man, when we saw ahead a wooden bridge at another narrowing. We were now in the Tobeatic Game Sanctuary, so we had to expect this. With only a cursory peek down under the bridge, we let the quickening black water take us and away we went, mostly just steering, for a kilometre at most, when we turned a corner on flat water to come upon a well-constructed framed cabin. This was the Department of Natural Resources camp we had been expecting, but it would have been nicer to meet a log cabin instead of this building on a concrete block foundation. It sure took away from the naturalness of the whole scene, but it was to be the only corruption by man we saw in this wild and pure country.

After a brief look around the site, we continued along another long section of easygoing rapids, then entered flat water and country different from any other we had passed through. Titus Smith's description almost two hundred years ago still applied to the scene. From his report of his "western tour," although he doesn't give it a name, we know he exited, by foot, this river and entered Lake Rossignol, which he did know by that name. He wrote, "We have seen about 150 acres of good, wild meadow on the River and Lake, perhaps three hundred of poor which might be worth mowing. There may be more back, but that which lies off the lake is chiefly bad."

These meadows of blue-joint grass forming wide margins along both sides of the river felt nice and firm underfoot, although the spring melt that had preceded us in April likely overran the land back then.

By now, the Shelburne had pretty well run its course, having gotten just about down to the level of the Rossignol, but there was one last tumbling turn it had to make to give us one last chance at proper canoe handling, which we were finally beginning to master. When we coasted onto the last of the Shelburne and made a sharp turn to the right, we were presented with a vista of tree stumps and rocks, and, in a stand of white pine, a most curious object.

Here was a large boat, nestled bow-in, high and dry beneath towering pines and put there, no doubt, as succour to weary travellers—a curiosity to be found in such a place as this—a sturdy lapstrake craft, twenty-six feet six inches long, with its small pilot's cabin someone extended back to the stern, which was cut out for a door.

This boat once belonged to American writer Zane Grey.

This unique cabin can sleep two on bunks in the bow, has a small table and chair, some shelving, some pots, and a small cast iron stove with decorative scroll work and the words "Jewel Stoves and Ranges" showing through the rust. Any flat surface inside was written on—names, dates, comments, record of fish caught, and even one tattle-tale note with an arrow pointing down to the bunk. The earliest record I found was dated November 20, 1949, but there were many others too faded to read.

I have been told that this boat once belonged to Zane Grey, the American writer of outdoor adventure stories. He used to come to Nova Scotia through the 1920s with the grandfather of a friend of mine, to fish for tuna out of Liverpool, Nova Scotia. It is not known if this boat was used in the salt water for tuna fishing, and later transported up into Lake Rossignol, or if it was constructed on the lake. At any rate, it was equipped with two 1928 Chevrolet engines, and very probably was used for towing large log booms across the lake to the outflow into the Mersey River. It has been kept watertight and is generally maintained by the Annapolis Valley Paddlers.

Leaving the river to tackle the six miles of Lake Rossignol wasn't without a twinge of regret—we knew we would not likely ever travel its far reaches again to live in its wild beauty.

The tree stumps we wove through and the wide vista of rocks and islands were in stark contrast to it. The name Rossignol is just about the oldest for a lake in Nova Scotia, named by Champlain in the seventeenth century after a Captain Rossignol who traded for furs at Liverpool. Now twice as large in area as it was prior to 1929, when damming was first begun, it has always been a rock-studded body of water, and it didn't impress Titus Smith much in 1801 when he said, "this lake is not a regular valley filled with water, but a small concavity in a great plain of rocks."

We became a mere speck on the lake, but our minds were back there on the river. We felt part of its deep forest mystery, a wild country ever the reminder of a heritage we must maintain, one that holds its own stern codes, but we heard its demands and obeyed them. The tasks it set for us were often tough, sometimes harsh, we didn't complain but complied as we should have, and were rewarded for that, and will remain always the better for it.

PART TWO

A Liscomb Episode

A good Samaritan

A benevolent fate looking for someone to smile upon seems to be out there in the backwoods, otherwise how can you explain the laughter that accompanies every recounting of a woods experience—or almost every one. Perhaps just the fact that you got out of the woods is good for a laugh, but I suspect that the louder the chuckles the less humourous the episode must have been at the time—almost like a law of physics.

This was going to be a swell trip, one that I had longed to take, both because of the remoteness of the area where fishing was supposed to be great and because I wanted to visit and sketch an old warden's cabin to add to the sixty-odd I'd already seen.

My friends Doug and Eric had been to this cabin on Hunting Lake in the Liscomb Game Sanctuary a few years before, and were only too happy to make the trip again as well as help me in my quest to capture on paper as many of these old cabins as possible before they collapsed into heaps of rotted wood. We weren't hobbling ourselves to a set time frame for the trip—if we stayed in four, five days, that was okay. We were just going to enjoy ourselves exploring the Liscomb River system, taking one day at a time and soaking up as much as we could of the wild surroundings there.

As the guest, more or less, I was told I needn't bring cooking or eating utensils—the others would look after those requirements. I could even spare on food, since Eric was going to prepare three gourmet dinners for us—something he liked doing when making trips like this. That suited me just fine—less to carry, although I wasn't quite sure what carrying I was going to have to do. Despite those kind allowances to me, when I saw the packs and paraphernalia the guys had loaded on the eighteen-foot aluminum freighter canoe, compared it to my meagre, cut-down simple bundle, I had to ask myself whether I'm too stingy to spend money on fancy equipment and extra foods (that I might actually enjoy having), or whether I had an instinctive need to conserve energy in case I needed it to get us out of a jam. Observing my companions, I wondered if perhaps I could do with some new imprinting—if the old genes were up to it, that is.

The day dawned bright and warm in this late May, as we bounced along secondary roads, with me keeping a wary eye out the rear window of the jeep to make sure that the gear in the canoe didn't come adrift. The topographical map 11 E/1 (Liscomb) (see next page) shows the dirt road, labelled Seloam Lake Road, going northeast to Big Brook Lake, where we stopped to look around at the remains of old operations—likely a sawmill, although the presence of quartz and small mounds, which were probably old tailings, seemed to indicate gold prospecting on a modest scale, as there was no evidence of any shaft work. With the remains of a pier or loading dock still evident at the site, there must have been lots of activity going on there for a good number of years, although a map of this area produced by the Geological Survey Department of Canada in 1895, which is amazingly accurate when compared to a modern topographical map, shows no activity of any sort at the lake. In fact, no trail or tote road goes near the lake, even though many are shown elsewhere in the area.

E.R. Faribault and Hugh Fletcher were assigned the task of surveying the geology of Nova Scotia, from the 1880s and into the turn of the century. The results they produced were prodigious, considering the remoteness of the hinterland in those days, when most travelling was on foot. These men had "the right stuff." When you see a camp marked on a lake or stream, you can only shake your head and wonder how they could possibly have gotten back there. But you have to realize that Faribault and Fletcher didn't necessarily see a lot of what you see on their maps; that would have been impossible.

In studying their maps, you can get a pretty good idea of where these men actually foot-slogged, and where they didn't venture. The maps have lines traced longitudinally all over the

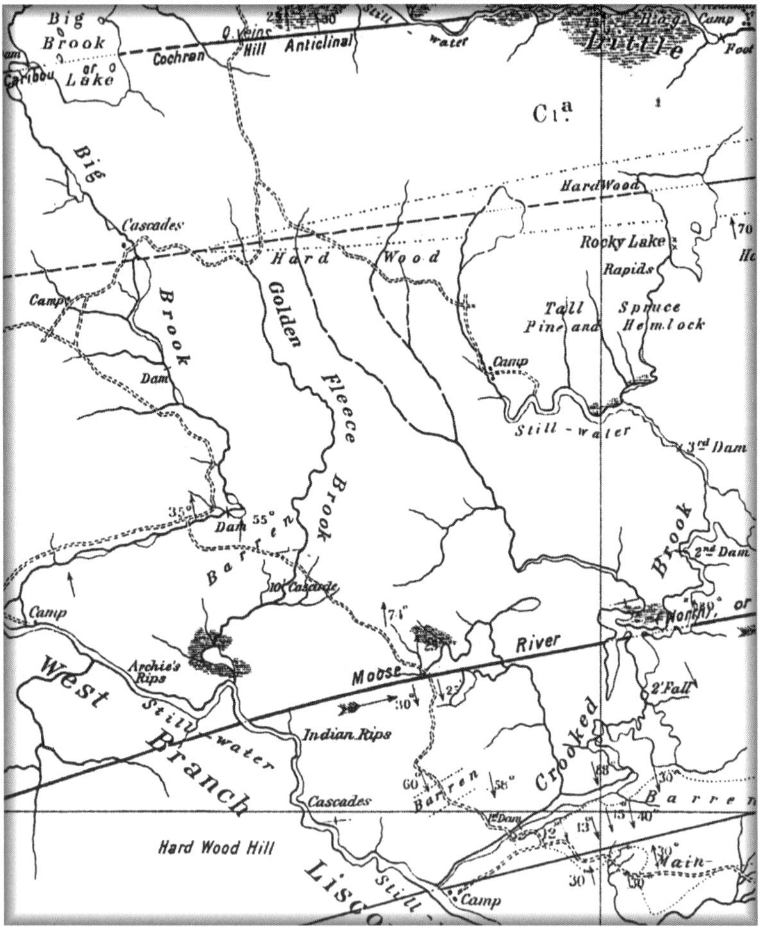

1895 Geological Survey Map

face of Nova Scotia, except for the southwestern part, which they never did get to survey. The lines they represent folds of rock strata forming ridges.

A solid line means that the route was followed or traced, a broken line means the route wasn't traced—they had to do a lot of guessing, which is only reasonable. Big Brook Lake, where we stopped, is in the upper left hand corner of the map. Judging from the broken line, Faribault didn't touch the lake, but he did actually trace its outline by working in from both sides of a wood road (double dotted line), shown to the east of

Big Brook Lake. I was particularly interested to discover that he was actually at two points on the Liscomb River, which we passed (on the map two solid lines cross the river). We'll be bumping into Faribault a couple of more times later on in this narrative.

* * *

After taking a few photos at the lake, we were anxious to get on our way, even though it wasn't yet eleven o'clock. We were hoping to get some fishing in before settling into the cabin for a dinner about which only Eric knew the details, although Doug and I had an idea it would be a pretty grand affair.

Leaving the lake, we took a narrow dirt road heading south. After a mile or so we got onto an even narrower road where the tree branches snapped at our faces through the jeep's open windows. We were following the watershed that supplies the Liscomb River and descends two hundred feet over three miles, so we were continually going downhill, which in itself gives the impression that you're approaching something interesting.

We had gone about a mile along this narrow, sloping road, when we negotiated a sharp turn and were presented with a little gully where a small stream cut the road. Just as we began to climb up the other side of this cut, the jeep suddenly lost its steering. A quick look under the front suspension confirmed our worst fears—we had a broken tie-rod. Staring us in the face was the ultimate fix you figured you'd never get into.

The trip would have to be aborted. We'd have to walk to God knows where to get someone to come in and tow us out, and that would be some trick with the jeep facing the wrong way and nowhere to manoeuvre a truck, even if it could get in. Not even our winch with a hundred feet of cable was going to be much help here. Three despondent guys studying two front wheels that were hopelessly askew, but even in our despondency we couldn't help chuckling—those wheels looked so stupid!

Eric opted to stay with his vehicle, and Doug and I would go get help, probably fifteen miles away if we were lucky. So we packed some food in a small kit bag and began a journey we guessed would take us five hours, providing we could do three miles an hour. After an hour of walking, we arrived at the lake we had stopped at earlier to see if there might be somebody there. We waited around a bit, but it was clear this wasn't getting us anywhere, so we struck off again for a place

called Caledonia, which, according to our reckoning, was seven miles further on up the Big Brook Lake Road. Maybe this wasn't going to be as bad as we thought—only ten miles.

After another hour of walking and covering over six miles, a truck going in our direction came along, and naturally the fellow pulled over. In a predicament such as ours, you either hit the right guy or you don't—it's all got to do with the fate I mentioned at the beginning— and Ernie was fate at its sunniest. "Got a problem, huh? Aw, we can probably do somethin' for you—where are ya?" This good Samaritan wasn't talking about towing or something like that! He was talking about getting us on our way again and soon! I could hardly believe it! It didn't hurt our cause that Ernie had read a book I'd written which he found interesting; it made up for how dumb I felt about all that mechanical stuff.

Eric was one pleased fellow to see us back so soon—with help. The three of us watched Ernie go to work. He took out all a mechanic would ever need from his tool box in the back of his truck, including a propane torch, and in no time at all had the two pieces of the tie-rod off. Then he and Doug took off for Caledonia, where he was going to pull off a slick solution to the problem that only a practical man like him could come up with, especially out in the field.

Not more than two hours later Ernie and Doug returned with a piece of mechanical wizardry that put Ernie right up there with the geniuses of our age, at least in our estimation. He had slipped a length of steel pipe over the break and welded it to the tie-rod. Just as good as new! Not only that, he brought along a cooler full of cold beer. And his departing "Aw, just give me ten bucks for the gas," was the icing on the cake. You can imagine we settled with him for a lot more than that.

The atmosphere in that warm and sunny spot, without a fly in sight, on a road in deep woods couldn't have been more serene; it ranks about the most pleasant of all the ones I have experienced in the woods, made sweeter by having been plucked from the gloom of bitter disappointment and thrust into the sunny anticipation of good times to come. But our celebration had to end as all good times do, and we got back to the job at hand.

You'd have to be a whimsical character to come up with the names given to some of our lakes and streams. It's beyond even the most dogged efforts to explain some of them, because there is no written source to be found, and personal memories are pretty dim by now. The person who coined Golden Fleece Brook had to be a joker for sure. This name has been on the map since the early 1880s. Apparently Jason eventually located the sheep skin made of gold, but it was probably his long quest that the coiner recalled to describe some gold prospectors' fruitless efforts to find any gold on this brook (see map p. 54). Our little road ended here, so we launched our canoe in hopes of reaching the cabin by early evening. We'd lost a day's fishing, but we were darned pleased fellows, nevertheless.

Crossing much earlier footsteps

Golden Fleece Brook doesn't source from a lake, but results from watershed three miles from the Liscomb River. It's a healthy little stream in that it runs deep, but it cuts only a narrow path through peat bog for most of its length, and just before it reaches the river, it widens out into a pool.

What a sight it is, entering the Liscomb River at this point! A wide and deep water course runs at a rate to carry you along at an easy pace, and is heavily forested right to the water's edge. The water here was losing some of the momentum it had built up racing over Archie's Rip (we know from looking at the 1895 map that Archie was alive before the 1880s), so the nice, leisurely flow called for only an occasional steer of the paddle. There is a three-mile run down to Hunting Lake, broad, deep and black for most of the way, except for two sections where we had to get out and line the canoe through. It was after perhaps two miles with our four horsepower motor on low just to add a little extra push, that we came to the entry point of Crooked Brook. You will notice on the 1895 map (on p.54), that there is a camp there, and one of Faribault's solid lines crosses the river. In his report on this trip, he calls this camp Moose-bog Camp, where he undoubtedly stayed, and used the woods road shown on the map to get there. We stopped at the spot, but made only a cursory look-around, something I wish I could do over again. Knowing what I know now about Faribault's sojourn here, I would have taken the time to scour the spot and maybe unearth some remains of that old camp. The old map shows two structures and a road leading to them. At any rate, I feel certain I likely trod exactly where Faribault did. He reports in his notes that he didn't trace the syncline (folded rock strata), yet he drew it as a solid line, which indicates he did walk it.

Much more has been written about the geographical surveyors who surveyed the boundary between Canada and the United States, the Rockies, the boundaries of our western provinces and our northern lands, than about the geological surveyors of whom Faribault and Fletcher are two. But Nova Scotia is so small it has been fairly accurately surveyed by local authorities since the 1600s, so the geographical surveyors from Ottawa were not needed. But geology was another discipline, so we got Faribault and Fletcher. I've always been interested in the achievements of both types of our federal surveyors, because to me they personify the ultimate in physical and mental toughness paired with superlative character. They are real heroes! To give you an idea of Faribault's era of activity, he died in 1950 in Ottawa at the age of ninety.

We left that very picturesque spot where Crooked Brook enters the river, and continued along the final mile to our home for the next few days. The sun was getting low on the trees, mostly peeking through to cast long shadows across our bow as we entered a widening, and rode out onto, for me, fabled Hunting Lake. Just a few more yards and there it was—our cabin—but I was distracted by some mighty pretty activity on the water off the point across from where we landed—trout jumping everywhere! Boy, were we going to have fun!

When you approach a woods cabin, especially for the first time, you're all eyes. You really focus. You look at the door, both sides. You're suspicious, not sure what to expect. What'll you find when you pull that door open? Well, nothing darted out between our legs when we opened the door of this warden's cabin; everything inside was in order and waiting to provide comfort for the traveller.

Situated on a small knoll on the west side of the river's entrance to the lake (grid reference 518994 on topographical map 11 E/1), just inside the boundary of the Liscomb Game Sanctuary, the cabin was built in 1955 by Bill Jewers, his son Merle and Audie Parlee. These men have all passed away, but this cabin stands as a memorial to their craftsmanship.

It is 14'1" wide and 17' long; the door opening is 5'11" high. The door is always unlocked, so I don't know if that is a padlock under the weather shield—I've forgotten, even though

I drew it. Vertical construction where logs are not notched, unlike the horizontal style, gives better protection against rot, and allows for easier replacement of a bad log. There's a barred window on each side. That's a bench made of saplings in the front. In the back is a dug well neatly lined with stones.

Inside, the floor is made with wide groove and tongue boards. There are two log collar ties running from wall to wall, and the rafters are logs also. For a stove, there is a cut-down forty-five gallon drum with a flat surface. Against the back wall are two sets of metal bunks with board beds. A table, a couple of wood benches, a cupboard, a work counter and a firewood box complete the interior.

It was getting on to dusk, but I just had to get across to that narrow point of land where the trout were jumping. We had no bait, just our fly rods, so I tied on a #1 Mickey Finn streamer, and paddled the freighter over. Eric was cooking up a meal in his inimitable fashion, so there was nothing else for me to do.

Streamer flies are designed for use in moving water, especially in a riffle, where you retrieve the fly slowly against the current. In my experience, the Mickey Finn, with its sparse dressing of red and yellow hairs, never fails if there are any trout around. I no sooner cast out and began my retrieve when bang, I had one, and it was eager to get to deeper water, so I had great fun playing it carefully until I was finally able to net it. The daily bag limit for trout was ten, as was the possession limit at any one time. It looked to me as if the fishing was going to be really good, and that there would be lots of opportunity ahead for getting my limit, so I released this nice ten-incher—I'd start keeping selected catches the next day. I cast out again and brought in another nice fish—another catch and release. And a third one! But it was getting dark, so it was back to the cabin for steak and onions with green peppers, mushrooms and potatoes. Eric even concocted a treat with limes and rum.

No gold, but some trout

Hunting Lake isn't a picturesque body of water—except for part of its north shore, it is surrounded by marsh and bog a half mile inland in places, so it is wide open to the wind, offering practically no lee shore. Our cabin site had a northern exposure, which you try to avoid if at all possible when citing a cabin, but this one had to be inside the Liscomb Game Sanctuary, whose boundary followed the opposite shore. The sanctuary was established in 1928, and composes approximately two-hundred square miles of mostly remote country, although in degree of remoteness, it ranks third behind the Highlands National Park and the Tobeatic Wildlife Management Area. We were able to get a freighter canoe into here—you'd never get one into the Shelburne River, which flows through the Tobeatic, unless it was made of birchbark and you were voyageurs. To my knowledge, our cabin was the only one ever built on Hunting Lake. Loggers used Moose-bog cabin, where E.R. Faribault stayed, and floated saw logs down through the lake into the river, but there was no attraction for staying on the lake itself because it had no harvestable trees around it.

Our first night in the cabin wasn't quite what I'd been used to in woods cabins— flickering kerosene lamps or candles, and a wood stove for cooking basic fare. But Eric liked travelling in style. For starters, there was a propane stove and a propane lantern. The lantern reminded me of two brothers who once hosted me in their cosy old log cabin for a four-day fishing trip.They absolutely refused to use anything other than kerosene lanterns, because they couldn't stand the noise given off by a propane lantern, which, they felt, detracted from the peacefulness of woods cabins. I'm with them on that one. Then, of course, there was the gourmet meal and the cocktails that preceded it. Cocktails? My gosh, where am I? I found myself enjoying the extra little touches—the special condiments, the air pillows, the paper plates, (a frying pan was fine with me), and even soap packs and wet towels. But Eric was bent on enjoying himself to the fullest, caring not a whit about weight, or economizing on kit for easier management. Kind of infectious to tell you the truth.

In the morning it was bacon and eggs—whole eggs, mind you, with the yolk unbroken in the pan. I always thought you transported eggs broken in a container of some sort. Your choice of jam, grape jelly or marmalade, in their little plastic cups, on toast made on a wire contraption placed on top of the wood stove. I wondered why I couldn't have a dab of whipped cream on my coffee, but of course I didn't say anything.

I was going to leave that dandy little fishing spot across the way for later as we piled into the freighter canoe with Doug at the motor. The plan was to go down the lake to the river, and aim for Ladle Lake ten miles downstream, fishing along the way, and exploring the route. If we got too far to return to the cabin that night, we'd camp on the river overnight.

Now out of the sanctuary and going northeast, the Liscomb here is more like a continuous stillwater than a river. Ranging deep on both sides were raised sphagnum bogs with clumps of alder here and there. After a mile and a half, the river constricted at a spot called the Dreadnought—even back in Faribault's time there used to be a dam there. Faribault surveyed the vicinity and reported that the quartz present was likely gold bearing, although he didn't actually find gold himself. Doug didn't either after putting his prospector's magnifying glass to some pieces of rock.

Continuing for another mile, the river made a hairpin turn, where it was joined by a good-size brook running out of Island Lake a mile to the north. We took the turn, now heading south, and after a mile came to interesting crooks and turns; then the water split around a grassy island, running as short rapids into straightaway river again. The spot looked so inviting that we stopped to eat, fish, and even pan for gold, since Doug and Eric had also brought along their prospector pans.

I could adjust to kerosene and a compass being replaced by propane, and a global positioning device, but when I saw their prospecting pans, I knew I was out of touch. These weren't those metal pans you see in old Klondike scenes—these were high tech plastic jobs, one green and the other black, with ribs moulded around the sides, all the better for trapping specks of gold, they told me. These innovations sure took away some of the romance of gold panning, but after going through a few pounds of gravel with no sign of that tell-tale yellow, they decided to eat and fish instead. Now there were results!

What a spot this was! Each man had plenty of room to manoeveur—nothing to snare your fly on the backcast. And not only a Mickey Finn worked. I'd have one on and look over to see Eric's rod tip suddenly jerk and he'd be plenty busy. I heard Doug give a whoop more than once, so he was getting plenty of action. We were catching our supper, leaving us able to catch more tomorrow. Then all of a sudden everything was quiet. The trout were there, alright, but we had put them down with all the splashing and darting by their mates, and I was surprised it hadn't happened sooner. Maybe by tomorrow they would have forgotten.

Our minds now turned to a good waterway we had passed coming from Island Lake. We wanted to investigate that lake to see if we could access it, as it looked very interesting. So back we went, making a detour from our planned route. We prodded up the brook until we came to tumbling water, then got out and followed a trail up to the lake, but we could only stand on the lake's edge; carrying the freighter up there would have been just too tough. At least we were exploring. There was one interesting happening on that little walk, though. As I was leading the way up the trail I noticed something flopping around in the stream. A closer look and I saw three or four common suckers each with their bellies gone—a big bite had been taken out of them. So we had disturbed either a bear or a coyote having himself a good meal.

Disaster

After that detour, which put us back a couple of hours, we headed back to where we had had all that swell fishing, with the intention of continuing on to Ladle Lake. Although the sky was overcast, it was warm, and the run from Island Lake was calm, so here were three relaxed guys taking in the scenery and thinking of the good fishing ahead—and maybe even seeing something out of the ordinary, which you can usually count on when travelling the backwoods for a good period.

Oh, how you can suddenly be knocked out of your reverie and into a state you never thought was in the cards! A bear, a big fellow, just ambling along through the low brush bordering the river, and not yet aware of us as we rounded a point. It was so damned quick! One minute we were all eyes on that bear, and the next we were in the water, rolled over by a submerged rock. When I bobbed up I saw the beast stand up on his hind legs to survey the rumpus, and then bound off into the woods, probably chuckling that we got what we deserved for disturbing his meal.

It was a good thing for us that the waterway was narrow. Hanging onto the boat while scrambling to retrieve our gear must have been something to see. Our feet could just touch bottom, so we were able to get a purchase when grabbing at things, and finally got almost everything into the bushes where we could make a tally. Besides being divested of our high opinions concerning our woods travelling abilities, the toll was two ruined expensive cameras, one fishing rod and reel, and one of my rubber boots. One paddle we could see floating away with the current. And, oh yeah—our nice string of trout as well. Then, wouldn't you know it! Along came two fishermen in a canoe with our paddle offering their help. Sheepish! We tried to put a good face on it, thanked them, and wished they had never come along.

We removed the two plugs from the outboard and dried them, but that didn't do any good. We were getting spark but no ignition. Things didn't look good. We were five miles from the cabin, each of us probably weighed ten more pounds than before, and all the gear was heavier too, so paddling that canoe wasn't going to be a picnic. And now a stiff wind was starting to work up but at least we had three paddles.

For nearly four hours we paddled into the wind and rough water before we finally got to the warden's cabin at early dusk. Doug had figured out what had happened to the outboard. When the motor was submerged after we hit the rock, it ran for a moment or two and water got inside the chambers, so the pressure the pistons put on the head gasket blew it. So that was the end of that.

We had to make some sense of the sodden gear, so the cabin became festooned with wet clothing. We had that stove pumped up pretty high—the sides were getting cherry red, which you usually associate with a swell camp scene. But this was no lazy camp time enjoyed after a long day's fishing—just the cussed job of each looking after his own kit, with no time for leisure. It would have been nice to slip into a sleeping bag, but they had been dunked like everything else, so we made do with whatever pieces of dry clothing we had, and curled up on the boards on the bunks. I used a plastic bag stuffed with moss for a pillow, and tossed and turned into some pretence for sleep, spending most of my time shifting my body weight around.

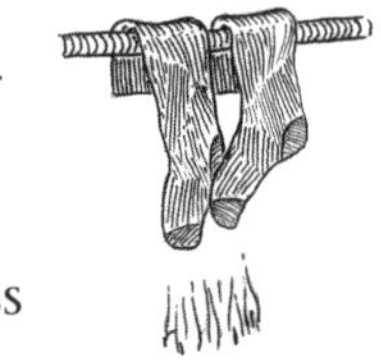

In the morning, Eric wasn't going to be denied serving up some bacon and eggs, so we had the typical aromatic camp breakfast, which we would be needing for the long up-stream paddle ahead of us. Gee, it was hard leaving this place. We slowly got ourselves together, and it was when I was putting money and other papers back into my wallet, now that they were dry, that I noticed one folded piece of paper I had purposely brought in to post on a wall for people to read—kind of a camp artifact you might say. It was a poem by an anonymous author that I had seen burned into a slab of ash wood and nailed to the wall of a cabin I once visited in Pictou County. I always liked it, and so include it in this narrative, exactly as I found it:

Beach wood fires are bright and clear if the logs are kept a year. Birch and fir logs burn too fast blaze up bright and do not last. Elm wood burns like a church yard mould, even the very flames are cold. Poplar gives a bitter smoke—fills your eyes and makes you choke. Apple wood will scent your room with an incense like perfume. Oak and maple if dry and old keep away the winter's cold. But ash wood wet and ash wood dry, a king shall warm his slippers by.

-ANON

So we were leaving the same area that E.R. Faribault tramped around for a few days in the summer of 1886. He and four assistants surveyed through Guysborough county from June 2 to the end of November, and made a detailed topographic and geological survey of the country lying between the

Liscomb and Sheet Harbour Rivers and the Atlantic coast. He reported that a map of the area would be ready for publication "next spring"; this map was actually the culmination of work carried out over a four-year period beginning in 1882. Of course maps were progressively produced by the Geological Survey Department of Canada through the turn of the century. To assist his mapping, he used maps produced by either the Nova Scotia government or by the local municipalities, but they were not as accurate as the ones produced through the efforts of men like himself and Hugh Fletcher.

Just to give you an idea of the extent of his travels in the bush, for up to six months or more every year, Faribault, on his 1886 journeys in Nova Scotia, reported he had followed 538 miles of stream and 130 miles of wood roads. He also reported that he measured many heights taken with the barometer. I don't quite understand how a barometer could give him vertical height, except if surveying in mountains like the Rockies, but at least it shows he was doing true topo-graphical-graphic surveying, where elevation is a key factor. Faribault wasn't given to reporting on camp life, trout fishing, or the inevitable sightings of interesting things, at least not in his official reports. Fletcher, on the other hand, made much mention of flora and scenic beauty through his travels in northern Guysborough, Antigonish and Pictou counties. Still, you can imagine the tremendously interesting and robust sort of life Faribault must have led. It reminds me of a good friend of mine who used to regularly travel his forty-mile trap line in the same general area and once said of him, "Oh my, that man must've been somethin''."

Leaving some ghosts behind

Back up the Liscomb we paddled in a slightly downcast mood because of the way the trip had gone, and the work ahead. Before we left the cabin I had posted a little note asking any users to please respect the cabin and the surroundings and not to leave any mess—"take your garbage out with you." I didn't expect that would be read anytime soon—weeks maybe—but my timing was off; on a turn in the river ahead two canoes with four men appeared. Weren't those chaps tickled to meet us! Now they had the cabin to stay in, and you can bet they weren't all that upset about our mishap. No wonder they gladly parted with two spark plugs that matched ours—what good we thought they'd do I don't know—especially when Eric, always well-equipped, gave them a pint of something strong in exchange. The other guys were well equipped too—several cases of beer were going to put paid to my little note for sure.

This was going to be a long paddle up into Golden Fleece Brook—a good three hours anyway—but we had an early start so took our time, and there was no wind, which made the trip unlike the damned grind we had had the day before. The fact that I sometimes had to step into the water with my camp shoes on, since I had only one rubber boot, was no bother at all. We stopped again at the outlet of Crooked Brook where Faribault stayed, and whiled away some time casting out a fly and walking around the shore, still unaware that there had been a camp here more than a hundred years ago.

Faribault and Fletcher did all the hard grind, resulting in the very detailed geological survey maps that covered most of the province, and which remained the only reliable maps of the interior of the province before the days of aerial photography. The coastlines that Faribault and Fletcher incorporated into their maps were done fairly easily—they had access to the admiralty charts that had been made from Royal Navy surveys since the early eighteenth century. Captain James Cook himself once over-wintered in Halifax soon after its founding, and charted part of Nova Scotia's coastline. These charts gave Faribault a good basis for his surveys, but it was the interior, the lakes and river systems where he had to do a lot of trail blazing. In his reports, he acknowledges the assistance of many men—locals who were largely trappers and

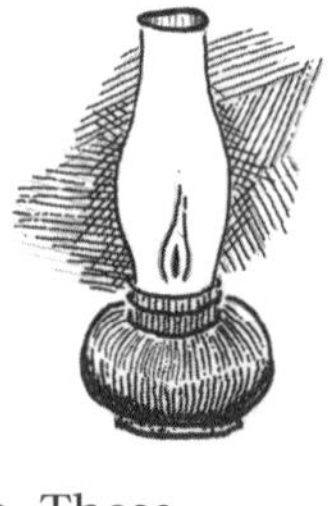

woodsmen and who sat with him by candle light or kerosene lantern tracing out on paper the country they knew like the back of their hands. Their input was invaluable for producing accurate maps, as were the Church maps.

A.F. Church was the first real mapper of Nova Scotia, using a scale much larger than had been used by previous map makers. William MacKay drew a map called "The Great Map of Nova Scotia," which was produced in 1834 by C.H. Belcher of Halifax, but it gave almost no detail of the interior or the southwestern, eastern and Cape Breton parts of the province. The scale he used was one inch to ten miles. Church's maps, although showing many blank areas, misplaced or misshapen lakes and streams, and even imaginary lakes especially, again, in the southwestern part of the province, nevertheless gave much more detail of the interior and were a great help to Faribault.

Church, an American, moved to Halifax during the American Civil War. He had experience as a surveyor in Maine, so right away presented himself to the Nova Scotia Government as a mapmaker and publisher. In 1862 the government had started negotiating with a surveyor to produce a map of the province, focussing mainly on the townships, but the fellow died, so Church stepped in to fill the void and, in 1865, started producing maps, county by county, on contract to the government. It took him twenty-three years, from 1865 to 1888, to produce maps of all eighteen counties. On the following page are two maps covering the same area of Guysborough County—one by Church and one by Faribault.

Church's map of Guysborough County was published in 1876, and Faribault's in 1895, although the latter was finished by 1886. Clearly, Faribault benefited more from the input of local people than did Church. Hunting Lake on Church's map compares well with Faribault's in shape, although it is not named, and neither is Island Lake, but they must have had names back then, especially when Faribault antedates Church by only ten years. Church probably missed out on those names by not sitting down long enough with the people who

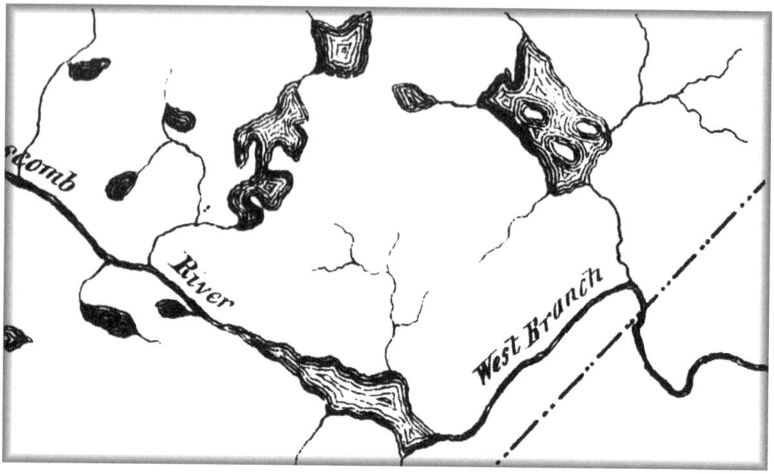

Church's map

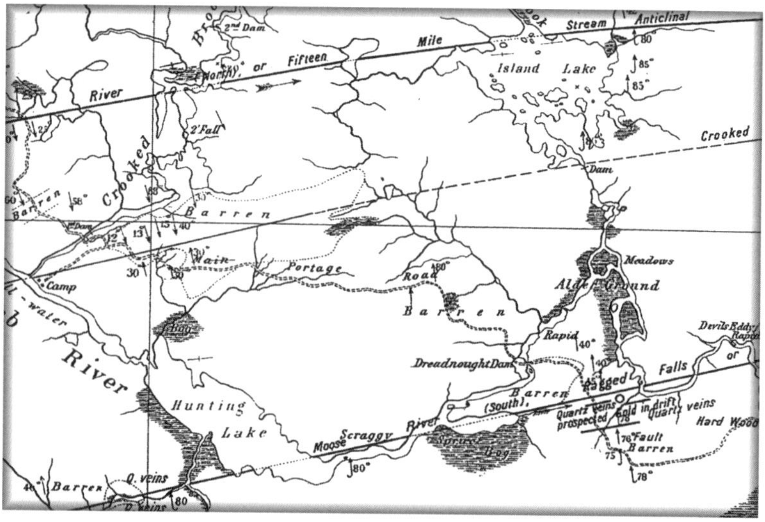

Faribault's map of Guysborough County

travelled those woods. (Faribault's map here connects with the one shown in Part One.)

We dallied for a while at Crooked Brook, where I experienced quite a thrill when I netted the largest trout I ever caught—a seventeen-incher, which I had no means to weigh, but which we figured must have been at least three pounds. I caught it on a Muddler Minnow that I first squeezed the air out of (the deer hairs), and soaked in mud so that it would run below the surface as I slowly reeled it in. Here was a bit of a break for a change, but since I didn't want it to get around that I came off a great fishing trip with only one trout, I released it instead. If anybody wanted to know what we were doing, the official line was that we were exploring for gold; didn't even wet a line.

Faribault certainly saw Golden Fleece Brook but probably read no particular inference in its name, while we identified ourselves with Jason and the Argonauts—quest through hardship—except they got their fleece. Arms and shoulders by now were getting pretty tired after hour upon hour of paddling over the last two days, but entering that brook somehow eased the pain as we drove to the finish line just as it began to rain. We had passed through some of the province's oldest history, and maybe we added a little bit to it ourselves, for anybody reading this a hundred years from now. The name Liscomb has been attached to this part of the province since the early 1700s, even before Captain Cook cruised along this eastern shore. The name might come from Liscomb House, a Tudor mansion in Buckinghamshire in England, but nobody knows for sure.

The rain was getting heavier as we nosed into the landing where our jeep was, and since our rain gear was packed away somewhere and we were too tired to dig it out, we were getting good and wet, but were just happy to be out and on our way.

With any good story there's a finale, and it just so happens that this account too has a capper: I was attacked by a great blue heron. We were snaking our way along the narrow road, when a large bird flew along the road ahead of us, then landed. As we neared it, and saw it was a heron, off it went

again, but it wouldn't leave the road. This was a strange place for a heron to be, and the thing couldn't seem to gain altitude. Rain or no rain, we were going to get that fellow oriented properly, so out we got, and when we approached it, it walked into the woods. So in we went too, and soon realized we had one tough customer on our hands. One look at that five-inch dagger of a beak ready to strike made us plenty wary, and when Eric moved up behind to try and grab it, it made a hissing lunge at me. I put up my hands to protect my face, stumbled backward, and beat a fast retreat. That was it for us! It wasn't until we were back in the jeep that I noticed blood dripping from my left hand—lots of it—and the skin ripped off my left thumb knuckle. Was it a branch or was it that beak? You can guess what my version is.

PART THREE

Four tales of backwoods travel in winter

A derelict

A field test

Forerunners

After a January thaw

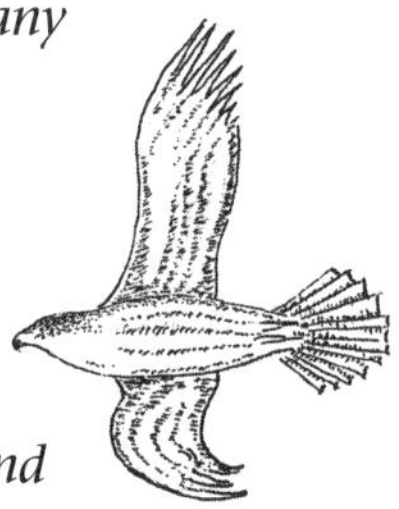

What follows here are the accounts of four winter trips I have made with friends. I chose these as being representative of the many I have made, but I regret my narratives can't compare to actually being there with us. Their telling brings up a lot of memories, and gratitude that we had the privilege to be able to travel like we did; for the physical challenge, as well as the soul-stirring impressions of passing through crystal bedecked woods and lakes, where sharp, crisp air, and stunning, sparkling night skies are the norm. This is what makes winter travel through Nova Scotia's woods an invigorating experience. These accounts are meant to inspire interest in wintertime travel, while also providing some tips on how to carry it out.

A Derelict

Just before we put our snowshoes on to begin our trip, we left the trail to look for something Doug wanted to revisit after seeing it some years before. There it was—a lonely headstone hidden by bushes and trees, hopefully not Godforsaken, but it certainly was about the loneliest burial spot I've ever seen.

In Memory
William Trimble
Died May 4 1887
Age 57

If ever a person could set the tone for this two-day trip through the woods we were about to make, William did it. That feeling was one of being taken back a century or more when things were simpler. I don't know who William was or what he did, though he was laid to rest under an impressive three-foot-high sandstone marker with a scrolled cap artfully chiselled, and not much weathered except for some chips taken out by bullets. William had been lying in that lonely spot for 104 years when I visited him, and thinking about him put a certain stamp on the trip.

There was a heavy snow cover where the trail was open to the sky, although passing through thicker woods it wasn't that deep, but we left our shoes on anyway for the next deep stuff. My snowshoes were the old standards—the ash and moosehide type—while Doug's were made of aluminum with nylon webbing, and had built-in ice crampons built in as well. These modern designs are very effective, especially with their harness and ice-gripping ability, but we both agreed that my old type had more surface area than his, which made them better at keeping you aloft in deep snow. For a while we followed an old woods road, then branched off through the woods to take up with a brook leading to the first of several lakes we would be crossing. It was when we hit that brook that I had a once-in-a-lifetime experience. This brook had earlier flooded its banks, leaving the surrounding low land covered with ice throughout an alder stand. Here we startled two beavers, who began walking as best they could on the slippery surface to open water. They couldn't manoeuvre very well, so as one passed by my feet I instinctively bent down and patted it—and it didn't react in the least, which surprised me. Patting a beaver in the woods is something you just don't get to do, but I did have that privilege, and my only reaction was to how coarse the fur felt.

Although this trip was only undertaken to find out whether or not an old cabin Doug and I knew of would be usable during the fishing season, it has since represented for us a movement back to a time when there seemed to exist a refinement of behaviour you only glimpse today—when you weren't harried into all types of the neuroses that seem to drive people nuts. That feeling was not only enhanced by the completely wild state of the country we were passing through, but also by something as simple as a map—a very old topographical map.

Leaving the beavers to their bank dens, which we noticed they avoided entering, we pushed our way along Rodgers Brook for a kilometre, sometimes through the most cussed of tangles, to finally break out onto Preston Long Lake. Here the snow was being whipped off the ice by a gale-force wind, and with the overcast sky we felt as though we were walking into the teeth of a blizzard. We could feel the resistance of our sleeping bags on top of our backpacks against the wind; when we entered the woods again after a mile out in the open, the release from that pressure was a welcome one.

It was an untracked half mile to the next body of water, Loon Lake, which passed through a bit of history as well, although if you weren't familiar with a topographical map of the area of fifty years ago, you wouldn't have known it. Somewhere along our passage our snowshoes crossed where horses and oxen once hauled logs out to East Preston. We think we saw the remains of a hauling road, and assured ourselves we had crossed Wisdom Old Wood Road. It's unlikely there is anyone alive who has an inkling of the origin of the name. North of where we were travelling is Lake Williams, and the old map shows Wisdom Old Camp, where lumbering went on through twelve months of the year. The map included here illustrates what I referred to earlier as a refinement of behaviour, in this case one of artistry.

This section of some of the country Doug and I passed through is taken from a topographical map produced in the 1940s. I have several of these and I value them highly, simply because of the artistry and detail put into them. For instance, there are twice as many contour lines as you'll find on your present-day topographical maps, and that's because they represent twenty-five-foot changes in elevation, compared to fifty feet today. That's called vertical interval. The artistic presentation of water in the lakes—drawing in all those lines contoured to the shoreline (called repeated shorelines)—must have taken a long time. You wonder if that was really necessary when blue ink used today for lakes would have been sufficient. But that's how they liked to do it then. Modern topographical maps show green for forest cover. Not the old ones! Some young draughtsman with the Army Survey Establishment labouriously drew in deciduous and coniferous tree symbols, even through he probably wasn't representing

1950s map showing elevation

the forest cover as it really existed, but that's okay— the eye appreciates an attractive presentation. Also, what I like about the old maps is that they show the elevation in feet above mean sea level on most lakes. Modern maps don't. In the old map, the elevation figure on Lake Williams just above the work "lake" says "200." Other details on these old maps are absent on the later ones, such as camps, trails, and dams. So here you have a nice example of how people years ago were interested in creating something artistic as well as informative—sadly missed today, I'd say.

That section of map shown here was printed in the early 1950s, but it was taken from data assembled much earlier. It resulted from surveys compiled, drawn and printed by the Army Survey Establishment of the Royal Canadian Engineers between 1917 and 1923. Those are the years when some young engineer sappers did their artistic work. But the R.C.E. weren't the true originators of these maps—they had access to previous work done on map making. The Geological Survey of Canada had done much earlier work, real footwork by men such as E.R. Faribault and Hugh Fletcher, to whom I have earlier referred. The Army Survey Establishment used their trailblazing, but had the benefit of newer technology, especially that of aerial photography carried out by the Royal Canadian Air Force through the late 1940s. Our present topographical maps are the result of all this effort over the past hundred years.

We left behind the faint remains of the Wisdom Old Road and, after some groping around, came out onto Loon Lake and the full blast of the driving snow again, which called for some hot tea and a bit of food, so we got in out of the weather under some tall pines to melt some ice, and were surprised to find the remains of what had once been a shelter made from lumber and plywood. The halt was a quick one, though, since we weren't getting much relief from the wind where we were, so we headed back out again for the goal of the cabin we had come to see, where we'd enjoy some warm comfort for the night.

This country is very wild, even though it is not that far from suburban Dartmouth. It's a box of territory 340 square miles, where no roads probe, except for maybe two rough ones, which can barely be negotiated by a four-wheel-drive vehicle with a winch. The land is bordered by the Waverley Road, the Old Guysborough road, the road from Musquodoboit Harbour to Meagher's Grant and the old number seven highway. Hopefully it will remain a pristine chunk of the province providing natural wildlife habitat as long as we have enlightened politicians who understand the value of such a natural resource.

When we reached the end of Loon Lake we followed a stream coming down, which flooded part of our passage, forcing us to take a wide detour. Here we could see the remains of an old log-driving sluice and a dam still partly held together by ten-inch spikes, and some indication that a road passed over that dam—the Wisdom Old Wood Road. Finally we got ourselves clear of this tangle of ice and fallen trees and came out to Tittle Lake and some easy walking with the wind at our backs. It was while we were making our way along that I noticed off to my left a remarkable sight, a cliff-like geological structure looming up into the air from the surrounding forest. You can easily pick it out on the old map. From the low surroundings of Tittle Lake, this rock structure rises two hundred feet like a monolith, and with the contour lines so close together, you can easily get an idea just how steep the sides are, something not quite so evident on modern maps, with their vertical intervals of fifty feet. The Army Survey Establishment put in these tight contour lines for obvious military purposes, which are not really needed in this day and age.

The low-lying land surrounding Tittle Lake changed abruptly as soon as we walked through a narrows to enter Byron Lake. Here the land rose steeply on all sides, including the monolith. Now we passed into the Waverley Game Sanctuary, which has an interesting history. In 1926, three thousand acres south of the Old Guysborough Road were set aside as a preserve for Boy Scouts to camp where they wouldn't be in any danger from hunters. Then in 1929 the area was enlarged and given its present name. This sanctuary is as pristine and wild as it ever was. Only one road, if you can call it that, enters the preserve. The road enters the woods behind North Preston and is all but impassable in spots, when you need a winch to get out of mud holes burying the tires. When we neared the south end of Byron Lake we turned into the woods to look for our refuge; then there it was.

This accompanying illustration is not exactly as we found the cabin; we made an alteration to the structure soon after getting there—we put a mattress over a collapsed part of the roof. If the mattress looks stiff up there, well, it is—a sodden, frozen mass of stuffing. There's a notice nailed to the door, put there by the Department of Natural Resources only twenty-one days before we got there. It says that if the owners of the cabin do not remove it within sixty days of the notice, it will be demolished, and a fine of five hundred dollars will be levied against the person who erected or uses it. I got a kick out of that one because it bore the signature of a friend of mine who

was a conservation officer of the department. For sure, Art didn't walk into the site like we did—the lucky son-of-a-gun flew in by helicopter. This tarpaper shack was built in more recent years on the spot of an earlier log cabin built in the 1940s by men known to Doug. Half of the tarpaper has been ripped off, and it wasn't done by bears, unless they were trying to get a fire started in the stove.

It was now early evening. Across the lake above the monolith a full moon was rising, and the temperature was falling—it was getting damned cold. Stepping into the cabin was something to put the chill into you. The door had been wide open, so I swept out snow that had drifted in, with a spruce bough. The little wood stove wasn't far from falling through the rotted floorboards, and it had a dangerous list. A rickety table and two bunks covered with frozen masses of pulp completed the interior. The wall boards, where they hadn't sprung loose, must have shrunk over the years because there were gaps between them to nicely air out the place. A long-unused cabin always has quite a chill to it, which, I believe, has something to do with physics. Living trees, although dormant in the dead of winter, still give off heat energy, but not dead wood, which a cabin is made of. That's my theory, anyway. If you step into a cabin and don't feel that chill, this tells you that that cabin was used not longer than five or six days before, because the heat energy absorbed from the fire in the stove still lingers; any longer and the chill creeps in again. Well, this rotting misery of a place hadn't felt the cheer of a fire for a long time for sure.

You can stand bare hands in the open winter woods, but, my gosh, they stung inside this place as you fiddled with the cold iron of the stove, and stuffed inside the frozen bits of bog spruce left long ago by the last visitors. If there's anything designed to drain your enthusiasm for getting camp comfort, this is it. Candlelight was all we had by which to lay out our sleeping bags on those icy mattresses, and arrange our gear, but the only real solution was to get into our sleeping bags. The skimpy sleeping bag I brought along, trusting as I did to the cosy place we were expecting, might as well have been a shroud for all the comfort it provided. I think I must have sounded like Sam McGee did when he complained about the cold during his final sojourn in the Yukon.

Since my friend Art had already threatened to demolish the place, we decided to give him a leg up. By nine o'clock the shelves and bench were gone, by ten we had started on the bunks, and by the time that cold, full moon was at its highest, we had stuffed most of the two bunks into the stove. But for all the labour we put into it, you could only feel heat when you shoved your hand into the open door. Through the night and into the dawn we took turns at the saw, and when we saw the last of the bunks, we also saw the last of a place to put the sleeping bags—you wouldn't even consider the floor—so we gave up on that crypt of a stove and turned our bleary eyes to our food on the table.

If ever there was a time when hope gets dashed to despair, this was it. The eggs in the container were frozen, the milk was darn near crystallized, and the molasses could hold up a telephone pole. There weren't going to be any toasted English muffins, running with butter and molasses, to serve with the scrambled eggs we weren't going to have, and you couldn't ask the little one-burner stove to cook up that swell concoction, shivering as we were with hands so cold you could barely wipe the drip from your nose. But it could heat water for tea, and that was our breakfast. For sure, there is a divine being somewhere who came up with the idea of the tea plant, for if ever there was a brew that can uplift the weary and dispirited, tea is it. When we stepped out of that mould of a cabin we were eager to pick up the journey into the warmth of the forest.

The cold, spent moon was hitting the tree tops when we took, probably, the last of last looks at the site, wondering if my friend Art would have an easier job demolishing the place. Unless he reads this or somebody squeals on me, he'll never know I was the last inhabitant of that cabin. But, if he does, I might be assessed the costs in taking the place down, since we "occupied it." Some occupying we did! Heck, we'll just plead we were two travellers who got in dire straits and needed shelter. (Two years later Doug and I passed that way again and, sure enough, all that remained of the cabin was a clearing showing some charred wood, scorched trees, and of course, that cheery stove.)

Doug's ice-gripping snowshoes far outperformed mine on the two-hundred-and-fifty-foot rise of trail along a half-mile where such a path naturally ices up from running water. I was forced to hug the margin, where I could find softer going, and when we finally reached the top of our climb, I felt that short trip a lot more than he did. At the top we came onto an historic trail—the Old Lookout Hill Road. You can see it on the vintage topographical map. It shows as a single dotted line until it joins a double dotted line, which leads south to North Preston and north into the Waverley Game Sanctuary. That single dotted line pretty well says it all, for the road is nothing more than a footpath now, but through the nineteenth century it was a well-travelled route.

The Old Lookout Hill Road was first surveyed in 1809 by Theophelus Chamberlain and Titus Smith. They started at Preston and went through to the Old Guysborough Road. The Royal Engineers built the fifteen miles of road between 1810-1812 as a means of access to interior land grants and to the markets in Preston and Dartmouth. It was also the first road into the area of Goff, pre-dating even the Old Guysborough Road, which was then only starting to be pushed through. Lookout Hill, being the highest point of land in the area at five hundred feet, was used as a look-out station by the military during the threat of invasion at the time by the Fenian Raids of 1860-1866. The only evidence the road was once an important link between two settled areas are the occasional rock in-fills barely showing through underbrush and snow. At this high elevation, we could see far in all directions, and the strong wind coming from the north explained why all the growth up there was so stunted. I cut out a section from a one-inch-thick spruce and counted the rings—there were fifteen, double what you would expect to find in lower, protected areas. From this summit, then, we began a descent that would take us out to the settlement of North Preston.

Passing from the days of Titus Smith, and from the days of Royal Engineer sappers labouring beyond our comprehension, from those of William Trimble the unknown, and from the long-gone artistry of map drawings, we gradually entered into the present as we descended the Old Lookout Hill Road. Signs of man's waste and litter now bordered our way, and it wasn't long before it somehow seemed appropriate to remove our snowshoes. Then we packed up and left.

A Field Test

DAY ONE

Wintertime travel for us evolved from being a means for checking out new lakes for fishing and bringing in boats, to becoming an end in itself. It's the best time of year to travel if you just want to examine new country, because ice allows you to walk where you otherwise couldn't. Woods and waterways, draped in white and locked in ice, are at their absolute best by far. Strenuous physical activity has also got a lot to do with it; it's just plain good for you. If you're able to do it and you have the desire, then you shouldn't pass up the chance.

The start of this trip will forever be imprinted in my mind's eye: Briant in harness, pulling our moulded plastic toboggan over the smooth, bare ice of Little River Lake in the Ship Harbour area. The glare of the sun was blinding, and the white of the surrounding forest brilliant on this cold last day of January. This was to be an exploratory trip to two out-of-the-way lakes we might like to visit in the spring—the idea being to blaze a trail to them when sight ahead is not obstructed by any foliage, and that it's easier to get around when you can walk on ice.

Briant in harness didn't need any assistance on this slick ice, and the other guy walked ahead watching for any danger spots, which we really didn't expect to see in this hard frozen country. Crampons aren't needed when walking on level, bare ice—it's when you get a little dusting of snow that you begin to slip and slide. The wind stiffened your cheeks, but you knew that cold air was packing those red corpuscles full of oxygen. That makes you sharp. The eyes see farther, your hearing becomes acute—all the senses are alert, and seem to get bolstered from a sixth one as well. The deep, resonant booming of the ice sounded far off as it contracted from the cold, which is always a good sign, because it signals hard ice getting thicker. Sometimes you'll notice spots around the edge of a lake where the water isn't frozen, even during the coldest of weather, but the ice bordering them is thick. This is usually the result of some material having been dissolved in the water at that spot—the more dissolved material in water, the lower the freezing point gets. Salt water, for instance, needs temperatures a lot lower than 0°C to freeze, because of the dissolved salt in it. Where some of the water at these open spots floods over the ice, it is invariably stained a rust colour.

The passage across the lake was as effortless in the harness as out, leaving either man the freedom to gaze around as he pleased, but we were now approaching a half-mile trip overland to the next lake, so the one out of harness had to pitch in. Here we started up a rocky footpath that has been travelled since before the Europeans arrived, but it is still only wide enough for "Indian file" and, if it went through four good growing seasons without a foot being set on it, it would probably disappear. Many years before, a friend and I hauled my wooden boat up this path through deep snow, and there was only room to do it by keeping the boat up on its side. We came to a footbridge over a fast-flowing brook running out of the next lake, where one misstep on this shaky structure would have sent us high-tailing it out of there, but we managed to get the toboggan across after only one heart stopper. But what almost took our breath away was the icy artistry nature carved for us there. Here was ice sculpted into wondrous shapes atop the slenderest of crystal pillars, or cantilevered out over rushing black water, defying most laws of mechanics, and everywhere this fantasia sparkles with red, blue and green flashes of light.

Northeast Lake was still—we could pick out no movement of any kind, yet it wasn't quiet, with the rumbling cannonade of cracking ice coming from its frozen vastness a mile ahead as we strode out onto the ice for another effortless stroll. This lake was called Moccasin Lake a hundred years ago and, as recently as 1939 on a Federal Department of Mines and Resources map, and was probably assigned its present name in the 1940s. When we reached the main body of the lake, we

The cabin on Moccasin Lake

could see a cabin I was acquainted with across on the eastern shoreline, so we went over to check it out and have a snack.

This log cabin is as much a part of Northeast (Moccasin) Lake as are the rocks, so I am obliged to describe it. It was built by Mac Blakeley in 1920-21 on Crown land, with the lease being held by the Morse family since 1953. The cabin measures 32′ long by 14′, 2″ wide. The interior is divided into two rooms: the kitchen area and the sleeping area, which has five cots. The cabin is equipped with just about anything you'd want for a long stay. But it's the detail of the camp log—comprised of four thick volumes which are no longer kept on site—that makes your eyes pop. Every trip ever made there is recorded in detail—fish catches, weather, anecdotes—but what was probably most telling of this place was what a visitor from England recorded in the log after having caught his first ever trout on an artificial fly: "Canada was just like this in my storybooks."

Continuing up the lake at a leisurely pace, we realized we shouldn't push on to a further lake to make camp, since we might be short on time for both setting up and exploring, so we determined to stop at the end of the lake instead. And what a spot we picked! A stream tumbles heavily into a narrow and secluded cove where there is open, grassy ground—ideal for setting up a tent and having a good spot for building a fireplace. The ground here had only a light dusting of snow, which made it a lot easier for laying our groundsheet.

We placed a reflector sheet on the ground foil side up, then set up the tent on it. Since we have to keep gear to a minimum whenever we travel, we can't worry too much about soft padding such as air mattresses, but will use a half-inch sponge mat. Before I spread out the mat I lay down some newspaper first, as insulation. We use double sleeping bags, one inside the other, and a half hour before crawling in we fill a hot-water bottle and shove it down the bottom of the inside bag. Just before getting in, we'll eat some chocolate or an orange for the carbohydrates to generate body heat, put on a wool balaclava, and use our heavy jackets as a pillow—and even -20°C won't bother you.

Light inside the tent is just a simple candle lantern if you can suspend one from the roof, but in our case we couldn't, so we crawled into our bags when it then had to be turned off. Neither a fuel lantern nor a candle will build up any heat inside a tent that you can feel in very cold weather—you just have to have good double sleeping bags, a woollen hat, something in your stomach and you'll be just fine.

With the tent in place and everything ready for our return, we departed into ever more wondrous sights of a land locked in ice crystals. Our goal was to reach two lakes we'd never seen before, three miles farther in, and this meant crossing six other lakes before we'd even begin to probe into them. The snow cover in the woods was thin, so we left our snowshoes at the campsite. First we followed the brook, which exited at our campsite, for a quarter mile, then came out onto Boot Lake and its smooth ice surface, which resulted from an earlier rain and a quick freeze-up. Walking this ice was an education—as it is every time I am able to see down through its depth. Air bubbles in vertical columns let you see the thickness of the ice, and also show how ice crystals arrange themselves.

Water is funny stuff because it doesn't act like any other liquid. All other liquids—carbon tetrachloride, for instance—

freeze from the bottom up; the colder they get the denser they become, so they sink. But not water. As it gets colder and denser, it sinks for a while, but then does an abrupt turn-around. When it reaches 4°C it stops contracting and getting heavier, then suddenly begins to expand and get lighter as it nears 0°C. By the time that point has been reached, it has floated to the surface and become solid. This is called the anomalous expansion of water (deviating from the normal rule), and you've got to believe that there must be some sort of super intelligence somewhere to think that one up. It's great for all the creatures that live underwater, and me too, because I can't walk on water.

We took a stroll around Boot Lake and wondered about its fishing prospects. It filled a narrow valley with heavy surrounding forest rising steeply—you could imagine the ice-locked shoreline plunging to deep holes where trout would like to stay. We took a thin trail up to a small lake that has no name on modern maps, but is labelled Moose Lake on a geological survey map of 1897, which surprised me since the lake is hardly big enough to even warrant a name, and it doesn't even get a mention in the Nova Scotia Gazetteer. There are twenty-eight Moose Lakes in the province, and ten alone in Halifax County, but this one is a sort of forgotten child although someone, way back, thought it deserved a name. When you compare very old maps to current ones, you discover many name changes, and wonder how that happens. All of the old names seem to be okay as far as I can see, but they got changed nevertheless. This lake is now officially off the books.

We crossed the lake and again entered the woods, which were a sparse mixture of pine and hardwood, and there the floor had a thin cover of snow so you could see far ahead, and it was just that condition that made us spot a discolouration on the snow. We came upon a perfect example of the efficiency of coyotes. Deer hair was strewn everywhere, but nothing else except for one leg bone, which had some of the marrow licked out—no hide—nothing. Those smart animals waste nothing.

The next lake we stepped out onto was Squirrel Lake, exactly a mile long and running north-south. It is a good example of how most of the province's lakes were formed and oriented. Because of the slope of the land mass, during the ice age the covering glacier slid off to the southeast and south, scooping out alluvium-filled hollows, which eventually filled with water. Very narrow with steep rising softwood all around, the lake was interesting to travel, since you could examine opposite shores practically at the same time. We imagined how nice this lake would look if travelling it by canoe, and apparently it was attractive enough to someone to build a cabin on it. This is a sight you see all too often in our woods, and there's no amount of explaining that'll change the nature in some humans. The framed cabin was now a derelict, mostly collapsed onto all kinds of debris and garbage. On one of my maps I have pencilled in "a g.d. mess."

It was getting colder now, and there was a stiff breeze that penetrated my heavy wool pants. As I mentioned earlier, anyone interested in making wintertime trips, preferably overnight, might like a tip or two, so I'll describe what we wear. The general rule we use is five layers for the torso, four for the arms, and two for the legs. The torso is covered by a windbreaking winter jacket, a heavy sweater, a heavy work shirt, a thermal underwear top with long sleeves, and a short-sleeved t-shirt. If you've done some heavy sweating, you'll get the chills if you just sit around, so get the t-shirt off immediately and replace it with a dry one. I've done it many times, and the short period of frigid exposure is soon rewarded by dry warmth. Sometimes I won't wear the thermal underwear top until the evening when it gets colder and I'm less active. Thermal long-john bottoms with heavy wool pants provide sufficient protection for the legs. Head covering is a personal preference, and I always use a wool balaclava—pulled down for the really cold wind. Snow boots with felt linings are the standard, because if you break through ice you'll likely go in over them anyway—then you're left to your own devices.

Hand protection, again, is a personal preference, mine being cotton-lined leather work gloves, as long as they don't get wet, in which case I'll then wear wool mittens of the home-knitted variety. I always have both with me.

Next we took a wide trail to Rabbit Lake. Up to this point we hadn't been trailblazing through unbroken country, but were following a canoe portage route that some stalwart canoers take, but they are latecomers compared to our experience in this country. Canoers, by their very nature, are the best environmentalists, and never disturb the land they pass through, like some characters who think they like the woods—they don't like it at all. We crossed Rabbit Lake and walked down to Bear Lake, which was only a short hop, but this was as far as we would be going this day because we were running out of time to get back to our campsite. Our goal was still a mile and a half away through woods that were never tracked, so we would have to make a second attempt the next day.

Back at the camp the serious stuff begins—getting fed and trying to keep warm before crawling into the sleeping bags. What is normally effortless in warm weather becomes something quite different; even something as simple as lighting a match. Sometimes the difference between the easy and the difficult can be extreme, and if you've never experienced it, you'll have a real eye-opener. Shivering with cold causes you to exert a lot more energy than you should while trying to do something, so you have to guard against that.

It was dark at six-thirty, which makes it difficult to prepare a meal, but the first order of business was to get a fire going. It was now -20°C, so we got the fire blazing away, rigged a small tarp as a curtain to reflect the heat onto our backs, then found the time to sit before the fire. We'd had only frozen sandwiches and tea on the trail, so we heated up some packaged soup and defrosted some muffins by placing them on a hot rock. Buttered muffins? This is an example of how something simple becomes an effort—rummaging with bare hands through your

food bag for frozen butter, using your knee as a cutting surface, then finding a place to put those hard pieces while you try to cut your muffins in half.... I was eating the noodles out of the saucepan and foregoing the butter, washing the muffins down with hot tea, to keep it quick and simple. But Briant wasn't going to keep it simple.

It must have been in the warmth of his home that he thought this one up. Or he had visions of Big Macs dancing in his head. He was going to have cheeseburgers as delectable as you see in the advertisements. So out comes this plastic container neatly packed with two beef patties, two slices of processed cheese, two slices of tomato, some lettuce, sliced buns and little packets of relish and mustard—all frozen. Things don't fry nicely in a frying pan too hot to handle, with your backside cold and smoke in your eyes, but you'd have to be as cold as the ice itself not to sympathize with the poor dreamer when the patties broke up into crumbled bits and stuck to the bottom of the pan, and the other ingredients got spattered with wood ash in the container when one corner melted out. It was a losing battle from the start, but he soldiered on for a while, trying to combat the unrelenting force of nature, but finally threw in the towel and was reduced to hunching over a saucepan, like I had done, and joining the real world.

Camping in the winter woods with only a tent is the least means for offering relaxation—you just don't get any—so we were mostly kept busy walking into the surrounding darkness to cut firewood and keep up the cheeriness of the fire without which the place would have been a gloomy one. Radiant heat from a wood fire isn't much good for warming the body in very cold weather and, even though we had the tarp for a backdrop, we still couldn't get our backsides warm when we'd sit, so we filled our water bottles with hot water and threw them into our bags—we even used leftover hot tea when the water pot shifted and spilled some of the contents. When we crawled into our bags at nine o'clock, minus only our boots and jackets, the warmth down by your feet was as pleasurable a feeling as you could ever want, and we were soon asleep.

DAY TWO

It was the buffeting of the wind on the tent—the sharp snaps of the material—that woke us, and we were surprised to see we had been asleep for almost ten hours. Oh, when the body gets worked for twelve hours straight, it sure knows how to ask for a break, and it did. Lying now with our heads outside our bags, our faces kept getting sprayed with the frost being knocked off the walls of the tent by the wind, was enough to force us out of our warm cocoons and face the long day's work ahead. But it took a lot of spraying before we finally gave in and groaned ourselves out into the frigid air.

Early morning in the winter woods when using a tent or a lean-to is no place to expend energy cutting wood and making a fire—you don't need it. You need food and hot drink, so we pumped up our little burner and heated oatmeal, thick beef stew and tea, but this time I felt up to preparing my favourite woods breakfast—English muffins with butter and molasses. I first sliced two muffins in half with my hunting knife, poured some hot tea into an aluminum plate on top of the burner with my plastic container of molasses in it—Briant being downright unreasonable not to let me immerse the container into the teapot itself—and dipped in the butter to get it soft. When the molasses and butter were warm, I scorched the muffins on the burner, and had myself a feast. Most of the fun you get from winter travel is keeping yourself fed and sheltered.

So it was back on the trail again, our goal being those two distant lakes we couldn't reach the day before, but were determined to reach now. We retraced our route and were again on Bear Lake. Here we followed the shore for some distance, then struck off into the woods for a quarter of a mile, to Crooked Lake. There was no careful compass reading required here—going due east was sufficient to get us to the lake. This is a fairly large lake, opened wide where we were, the ice showing the effects of a strong north wind; all along the south shore large ice clampers had been angled up three and four feet high, looking like some sort of crystal palisade. The loud booms from the pressure cracks sounded constantly as we neared an island close to the east side of the lake. There is a framed cabin on this island, and it's times like this we wished we had lock-picking skills to get inside, study our map, and have lunch with maybe a fire in the stove, but all we could do was spread the map out on the cabin platform and figure out how to reach Green Lake and Hurley Lake.

This required some precise compass work. Green Lake was only a third of a mile through the woods, but it was small, so we had to do better than simply choose one of the sixteen points on the compass if we wanted to hit the lake dead on. We'd have to use degrees instead, as well as factor in the declination for this section of the province. Any error on our compass march could easily send us past the lake to the north or south without even knowing. Compass or map declination is something not too many woods travellers are aware of. Experienced canoers take it into account, and that's because they're keen on woodcraft and also often make long carries where casual compass reading is not precise enough to get them where they want to go.

Declination means that the compass needle does not point to north on a map—not even close. The grid lines on a topographic map are taken from a reference point established by mapmakers. These lines don't point to either True North (the pole) or Magnetic North. The north-seeking compass needle does not point along those lines—it points considerably to the west of them when you are in the eastern part of the continent. Topographical maps show in their margins the declination, or variance, between Grid North and Magnetic North. This variance is given in degrees. The declination on the sectional maps for Nova Scotia ranges from between seventeen and twenty-two degrees west—the compass needle points anywhere from seventeen to twenty-two degrees west of the grid north lines, depending upon the section of the province you are studying. So when you initially align your compass north with the map grid lines and read the degree pointing to your objective, you must add the magnetic declination to that degree. If you keep on that corrected figure, you'll hit your objective.

So we figured in the declination for our route and walked into the woods. We advanced very carefully, stopping to take a reading and citing a tree on that line, then walking to it, making a blaze as well as a reverse one. The line we were following took us at times to impenetrable stuff that we'd have to skirt and, hopefully, get back on line again once around it. Later, if all went well, we'd be able to travel the route with some kinks in it for easier travelling. Perhaps after an hour of this slow work, we finally saw an opening in the forest ahead, and knew we had lucked in, which was a relief since it was now beginning to snow. When we walked out onto Green Lake, the snow was driving almost straight into our faces. It looked like we were in for a blizzard, but knowing we had a sure way out, we could take time to skip across to Hurley Lake, and even heat up some tea and have a lunch, because we were mighty hungry by now.

Since snow, when heated, gives only a fifth of its volume in water, I chopped some clear ice and filled my pot with it—ice only looses one-tenth of its volume when it becomes water. Briant went on to investigate Hurley Lake while I sheltered in some trees and melted the ice with my little stove; by the time he got back, the tea was ready. Snow was now driving in from the northeast in fine style to almost zero visibility, so our lunch was eaten huddled in amongst the trees. We didn't linger long since we had to get out and tend to another piece of business—storm or no storm—before we headed back to our campsite.

When we got back to Crooked Lake, instead of retracing to where we crossed it earlier, we headed up the lake to where we had a stove at an old campsite we used for fishing. We wanted to move the stove to a new spot—one that gave us access to better fishing. This added three miles of travelling before getting back to camp, but it had to be done now when we could take advantage of ice travel. Using a piece of canvas as a sort of toboggan, we pulled the stove a mile over ice that remained largely bare because of the strong wind. But by the time we got the stove to its new location, the snow was starting to build up on the ice, and with zero visibility we didn't find it any too easy to know where we should be headed. Just as a precaution, we tied a twenty-foot length of rope between us so we wouldn't get separated, and also because we couldn't tell if we were walking over weak spots or not; the rope would be a safeguard if one of us fell through.

Zero visibility from snow or fog on very large lakes requires using a compass, but Crooked Lake was small enough that our sense of direction would get us on familiar ground. It's an example, though, how travelling conditions can change for you very quickly, and how you should always be ready for that—we carry a compass at all times, even when covering ground we've travelled for years.

This white-out was the worst I ever experienced—I wondered if this is what the Inuit go through in the Barren Lands—and, even though it didn't last long, was a good lesson in being disoriented. We had begun walking, using our sense of direction, but soon got an uneasy feeling— like we had as kids playing blind man's bluff—and when I checked the compass, I discovered we were going east instead of northwest as we should have been, something that was hard for us to believe. Now this wasn't a life-threatening situation, since we would have bumped into land in a matter of minutes, but it could have landed us in a pretty pickle in some other territory.

By now, we were far off the track we'd come in on, because of the stove, and were on a somewhat different return route which was going to be much longer. We groped our way through the broken layout of the lake, sometimes catching sight of the woods, then again being in complete white-out, when we came to something very familiar—a short, rocky run coming in from Blue Woods Lake, one we had dragged a boat up and down probably eighty times.

I could never understand why this lake got its name, since the woods surrounding it have always looked green to me. The name itself is relatively new, as it doesn't show on a map of

1897. At any rate, we were making our way carefully up over the rocks and ice to enter Blue Woods, when we noticed hundreds of small, silvery fish swimming up through the frigid, tumbling waters to the upper lake. The sight was pretty amazing in this setting, locked hard in the grip of winter, when we think everything is in a deep sleep under all the ice and snow. We couldn't figure out what kind of fish they were as we watched them battling upstream against the water rushing down at them. Some irresistible instinct was driving them on, for sure. I later learned that these fish were land-locked smelt, a smaller version of the saltwater variety. This species, which only grow to about five inches, unlike their larger ocean cousins, spawn at night through the late winter and into spring, in fast-moving water. I feel privileged to come upon sights and scenes like this when travelling the woods. It's just one lesson after another.

The snow was still driving into our faces, but we were in closer quarters, so we could see where we were going. Still we tethered ourselves together again because this lower section of Blue Woods was treacherous with its many rocks at the surface, making the ice unstable.

We were soon off the lake and took a short pull-through to Bear Lake, and were now back on track to our camp, but what we passed through in the morning now looked very different because of the blizzard. When we finally got back to the campsite, it was late afternoon, but we decided to break camp anyway and head out, even though we had already covered ten very busy miles during the day. We weren't all that fresh to tackle three more miles pulling our toboggan through snow instead of sliding over smooth ice. And packing up all the gear takes time, which common sense should have told us we didn't have enough of. If there's one thing you should avoid, it's racing against the winter sun—it goes down awfully quick, especially when it's behind a thick cloud cover dumping snow on you. If there's nothing really pressing, make yourself comfortable for another night, then get out the next day in your own good time.

Trying to pack up neatly while the wind and snow is lashing at you makes you sloppy and slipshod—the tent can't fit into its bag because you only have time to bundle it up loosely. The upshot was that our four-foot toboggan got packed up in pretty bad fashion, so bad, in fact, that I had to carry some of my gear on my back. We now found ourselves in a race.

The next three and a half miles was the toughest trek either of us have ever had to make. Oh, we've made countless carries through the years under heavy loads that darn near sapped our strength, but the pace was slow and the distance was seldom over a mile. But here it was—ninety paces to the minute for a mile and a half down Northeast Lake before we could enter the woods, for starters. We didn't talk—just kept to the tedious swish-swish-swish as the sky got darker, and when we entered the woods for the half mile to Little River Lake, we walked into the night. "Good God, how careless to get ourselves into this dumb situation," I thought to myself, as we stumbled and fought our way along the rock-strewn footpath. In our distracted state of mind we struggled over the icy footbridge crossing the stream, caring less about seeing the fantastic ice sculptures that had stopped us in our tracks the day before.

Onto Little River Lake keeping the ninety paces per minute for another mile and a half, and I was wet inside with sweat. It was just about dark, and there was no hopeful contrast between the trees and the sky because of the heavy overcast, but at least the snow had stopped. The situation of not having a sky to help guide you is rare, but not uncommon, and that's why we had to get out the compass and read it by flashlight. A good point to remember regarding flashlights, is that those using smaller batteries, such as double A, won't work in very cold weather. That happened to mine the night before. I had to stick the two batteries inside my armpit for a while before they'd work, and then keep the flashlight warm in an inside shirt pocket.

As long as I was moving, I was keeping up my body heat, but in just that brief stop we made to read the compass, I felt the chill from my wet undershirt. I knew what was facing me at the end of the trip when we'd have to stop for a while—a bad case of the shivers and the start of hypothermia, something I had experienced years before, and remember as a very scary thing. And here I'm only talking about sweating, not falling in the water. Briant wasn't bothered with sweat like I was because of the jacket he was wearing; his was all wool which breathes easily—too easily for my liking when you're out in a cold, high wind—and lets the air pass through. My jacket was of a wind-breaking material that didn't allow for breathing. Both types have their merits, but his was by far the better design when you're doing ninety paces to the minute. Carrying my heavy backpack didn't help matters any. When we made another stop, this time to tie a rope on the back of the toboggan, which I would keep tension on for the half-mile descent we were soon to make down through the woods, I began shivering badly. That did it for me! I threw off my backpack, stripped to the waist to get rid of my wet t-shirt, got an extra one out of the backpack, and got all five layers back on again in probably thirty seconds. Any longer, my unlucky chum would have been like Cap toting the remains of Sam McGee through the Yukon.

Before I come to the end of this trip, I'd like to describe the refinement we made to our toboggan after this excursion. You could say we gave it a field test, and found it needed altering to meet the needs of the real world. This trip, by the way, was actually an aborted one, and that's because of the toboggan. It was fine for pulling on the level, but going through woods was just too tough, especially on the man in harness. We had intended picking up from our farthest point reached, which was where we relocated the stove, then crossing Tangier Grand Lake, and taking a very hilly and long hauling road out to the Mooseland Road. But that the leg scared us off because we knew it well.

Our toboggan is a tough, moulded plastic rig, four feet

long and eighteen inches wide. We added the handle with the plywood brace, to prevent lateral movement of the two arms, and it proved to be the real McCoy as we subsequently found out. Now the other guy could push, and also keep the apparatus from tipping over. All we needed now were some huskies.

As if it wasn't dark enough on the lake, entering that black tunnel of a woods road sure was. Briant had his flashlight up ahead, but it didn't do me much good, fifteen feet back holding onto the rope to restrain the toboggan. Going down this half-mile ice chute reminded me of Sir Ernest Shackleton and his men descending a huge ice field somewhere in the Antarctic, except that all we could lose was our dignity—if anybody happened to be watching. There was hardly a moment along this wild run when we worked together, with all the spills we took. The one I liked best was when I went shooting off on my back into the bushes, after my tether got loose, and the load took off after my unsuspecting chum, knocking him ass-over-kettle and dragging him thirty feet before both of us piled up against a tree—just about as fitting an ending as you could cook up.

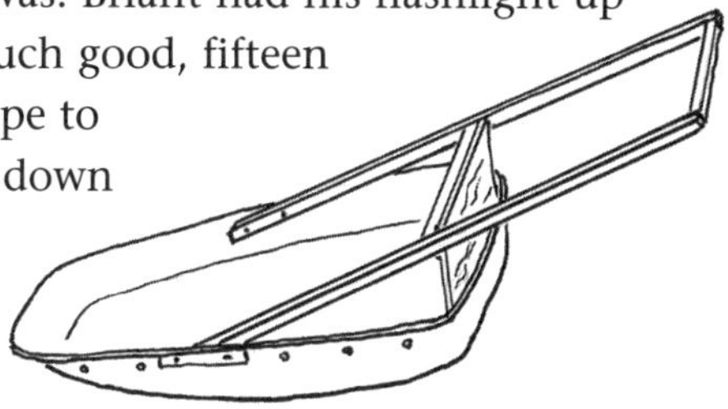

Forerunners

DAY ONE

Forerunners left their marks for us on this three-day trip into the backlands of Tangier one February. They are either presences you never get to see because you're not stealthy enough, or ghosts which you'll never get to see—maybe. Some are animals, but most are humans, and because their records are usually very old, a feeling of reverence comes over you as you stand quietly looking at them. Looking at all these marks is like stopping to smell the roses—you do it because they deserve the attention.

This was no trip where we could carry everything in on our backs; we were taking in a small stove, a heavy tent, a canvas tarpaulin, ice skates and a stovepipe, as well as the usual kit, so we had a two-wheeled cart for the job. The first leg was two and a half miles of iced-up road going thirty degrees uphill, then downhill. We had walked it a few days earlier to get an idea what we'd be up against, and without cleats, we knew what we'd be needing for this trip. Our cleats stopped our load from straining to go tumbling down the ice chutes, and gave us footing to pull up to the next crest—a hillier woods road you'd be hard put to find anywhere in the province. Just a word here about ice cleats: ours were the cheap type that fit in the instep of the boot and are held in place by only one strap. The shallower the instep, the more exposed the points of the cleats will be, and this is important when there is an inch or so of snow on the ice.

We were too late to catch one little drama that took place maybe just two hours before—deer and coyote tracks splattered with drops of blood crossing one of the crests. We resisted the temptation to follow their trail, and started down a steep ice hill with me in the yoke we had built on the cart, carefully grinding my cleats into the ice with each step, while Briant kept a strain on the handle on the back. At the bottom we reached mile one, and a fast-running brook cutting through the road to empty into a large stillwater. It was a struggle, and could have been a mishap with me still in the yoke, stepping from one icy rock to the next, while straining at the load, which Briant gamely kept from trying to dump me into the water. When we reached the other side we took a little rest, before deciding to do some sightseeing.

The ice on the stillwater was bare, so it was pleasant walking as we roamed around into other connecting still-waters. Now you can sometimes get caught up in what I call the prankish lure of the deep woods, when you imagine something that's not there, although unconsciously you may want it to be. We were crossing a narrow piece of land to another frozen pond when we heard whining—definitely an animal voice signalling distress, something like a rabbit does—so we stopped dead in our tracks to listen, then began slowly creeping toward the source. The whining continued, and we became convinced we were about to liberate an animal from a trap, or another animal. We stepped slowly and softly as we inched forward, peering through the trees toward the pond, but when we emerged from the trees we didn't see an animal in its death throes. We stood quietly listening and looking, when suddenly Briant pointed off to his left with a look of resigned disgust. There was an upturned relic of a boat locked in ice and some tall bog grass. The wind was whipping the grass against the side of the boat, making a scraping noise that hadn't the slightest resemblance to an animal's call of distress. But that's what happens when you're over-eager to see something different in the woods. Nature's prank got us that time, but on the way back to our cart I made a short detour into some woods to examine a rock cliff, when I was surprised to find my leg caught by some wire. On closer inspection I discovered a deer snare of heavy wire wrapped around a rotted and partly fallen birch tree.

Now it was back between the traces again, and another climb up an ice chute with the fellow behind pushing, and the one in front never being satisfied, always complaining he was either being pushed off balance or was having to do too much pulling. When we reached mile two we had to rest because the road played the devil with us going up, abruptly changing its mind, and not once holding to a level course. Half a mile to go, then flat ice for the next two days, and with our special cart working just great, despite our grousing, we were looking forward to some relaxed travelling.

As we neared the end of the road, we passed the collapsed remains of a once-proud hunting and fishing lodge, built by a businessman in the 1940s, before the road opened out to a sawdust-covered area marking the long-gone sawmill operation there. The site reminded me of an inspection of rivers of the province made in 1881 by Fred Vieth. His report cited over two hundred examples of sawmills dumping sawdust into the rivers, ruining spawning grounds for salmon, trout, gaspereaux and shad. The sawdust we were standing on had been lying here for forty years, and not a blade of grass was growing in it. This is because any nutrients that could nourish plants are not held in sawdust as they are in earth, and leach away.

We finally reached Bear Lake and what a sight it was! Smooth ice not marred anywhere by rough spots, as ideal a condition for a game of hockey as you could ever want. Like water, the ice took on the colour of the sky, so we dallied here for a while just admiring the azure surface, and imagining how far we could send a puck. And not a bit of wind! Here was the reason why anyone would toil into the winter woods—just to be there. As I mentioned earlier, we had packed our skates, but the trip across this lake to a short pull-through was less than a mile, so we didn't bother putting them on.

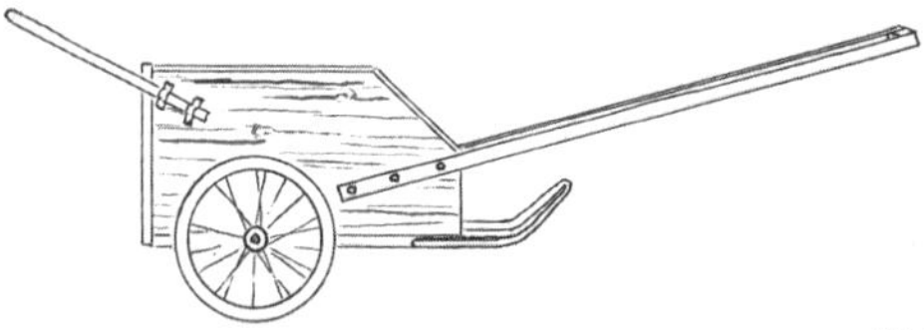

There was no toiling here, pulling the rig across the smooth surface—just time to drink in the scene and wonder if you could possibly be anywhere more pleasing to the senses. We had followed the original way into Tangier Grand Lake, used by loggers and sportsmen. We took the pull-through to Tangier Grand Lake and went to its only outlet, which has the remains of an old dam, to unload the tent where we'd be staying two nights from now. The old timbers that remain of that dam are a lasting memorial to Boyd Prest of Mooseland. He built a dam there in the 1930s to supply water power to a stamp mill for a gold-mining operation downstream on Tangier Lake. Then he built a second one at the same spot in the 1940s after the gold mine folded for a sawmill operation—the remains of which we see today. When we looked out on that large lake and saw slick, blue ice going off into the distance as far as the eye could see, we laced up our skates for the second leg of our trip.

Off we went, free as the breeze, gliding around islands and through passages, sometimes without the cart, just for the sheer fun of it. When we came to open water blocking our way, we went off separately, probing for a way out to the main body of the lake; something that would have been tiring and too time consuming if we had to do it on foot. The ease and freedom of movement that allowed us to glide over to investigate something as simple as a pressure ridge or a tree, put us in a kid-like state, open-eyed and carefree.

We finally found a way to bring the cart through and started the three and a half miles across ice, where the only sound was the noise of our blades crunching into the hard ice. On this wide expanse of ice, subject as it is to pressures from the wind, as well as to expansion and contraction, pressure ridges were even now being created, evidenced by the distant booming of cracking ice reverberating under our feet. Mile one of this crossing took us to a dome-like island in the middle of this expanse, and my thoughts went back thirty-five years or more to a tragic episode. Fishing with a friend near this island, we heard someone screaming, so we rowed as hard as we could towards the noise. We finally spotted an overturned boat with a man clinging to it—but his buddy had sunk to the bottom. I recall my friend and I probing with our fishing rods for the body, while the man hung on to our boat. As we passed the island, I could still identify the rock on the shore that we pulled the man to, and how he sat on it shivering and crying. As we passed by, I couldn't remember for the life of me if that body had ever been retrieved or not.

The next three miles were uneventful, with no forerunners to distract us, but a good breeze picked up at our backs and sent us easily along without moving our feet. We held open our coats like kids, and were sent sailing along for about a mile. We lost the wind behind a promontory of land, so went back to skating, and finally came to a roughly indented and rocky shoreline that grabbed our attention. For the last kilometre, we entered a twisting route through a bog, and neared the place in the woods where we would have to embark carrying everything on our backs because the trail was just too rough for the cart. The ice along this meander was crusted with snow, so we put our boots back on for the final stretch, stopping only to put our ears to a beaver lodge and listen to the whimperings of the kits inside. When we reached the stream spilling out into the bog we stopped for a mug-up and something to eat.

Although we lucked in with perfect weather conditions for ice skating, not having snow did rob us of seeing animal tracks. Ice on paths, however, will often show imprints, and it was while we were sitting on rocks by the path that we noticed imprints made by an animal, but not by feet. These were lines gouged across the ice like tiny trenches. I knew how they got there, but quizzed Briant, who couldn't come up with the answer. When deer mice and the like have to cross an open spot in the snow, they make little tunnels under the snow so they won't be spotted. These tunnels had gotten flooded by rain, then froze. We finished our lesson in natural history, and our lunch, then loaded up with the stove and all the gear to make for the lake and stay the night. Actually, there was too much gear for one carry, so I walked the trail three times to bring up the extra stuff. Since it was getting into early evening and would soon be dark, we were darn glad to drape the tarpaulin over our A-frame of poles with a bunk along each side, and set up the little wood stove.

The finishing touches to a campsite are always fun to do. The stove had to be at the right level, and the stovepipe angled just right. The nails above the stove to hold a line for drying clothes had to be in the right place, and...well, you know how it goes. By now it was dark, and we could really feel the cold, so we got a fire going in the stove and got some light on the subject from a small kerosene lantern stored here during our earlier trip when we built the A-frame. We were surprised how well our canvas tarp held in the heat from the stove, making as cosy an atmosphere as you would want, with the flickering light from the lantern casting looming shadows on the canvas as we busied ourselves heating beans, thick stew, and tea. Thin sponge mats were our only padding on the sapling platforms for our sleeping bags, because the moss we would normally use was frozen too hard to collect, and we were too lazy to go out in the dark to cut spruce boughs which, to tell the truth, I never found that satisfactory anyway. Our stove, to clear up any ideas here that we lugged in a heavy cast iron one, is a sheet-metal box seven inches square on the front and eighteen inches long, with detachable legs—a pretty light affair, and just the ticket for what we needed. At -22°C, it was new to us not to be throwing a hot water bottle into our double sleeping bags; as long as we had some good head covering we were going to be plenty warm.

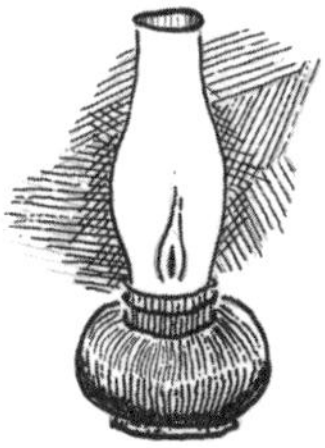

DAY TWO

It says something about your frame of mind when you wake up in the morning and can't decide whether to eat first or go skating. That's the simple decision we had to make when we opened the tarpaulin to let in some light and see what it was like outside. We had a south exposure, and the sun was just beginning to shoot in through the trees to our left, sending long shadows out across ice as smooth as glass, which was just waiting to send us gliding effortlessly to all parts of the lake on an inspection tour, but we decided to have a good breakfast first.

Snow sure beautifies a woods setting, and puts you nicely aloft of the tangle of lambkill when you are on snowshoes. But it gets down your neck and can be a nuisance in other ways. Ice alone, thick and smooth, is the ideal condition for winter travels. And being able to skate on it, too—what a bonus! So as soon as we finished our oatmeal and some hot cocoa, we laced up the skates and raced out on the lake, cutting tight corners clockwise and counterclockwise, going backwards as if defending against an attacking player, then easing up to just glide anywhere our curiosity took us. Paul Lake is broken up by several coves, and cruising along the shoreline where a couple of strides sends you coasting for a hundred feet was nothing but pure enjoyment. This trip ranks number one with me of all the winter trips I have made. You can bet re-living all this kid stuff has everything to do with that.

We found signs of two forerunners. A mile down the far end of the lake we came upon a granite boulder on the shore with a heavy eye-bolt embedded in it. It took a lot of pounding with a cold chisel to make the hole for that bolt, probably used to anchor a log boom. The bolt was imbedded in lead which, on some far-off day, someone melted over a fire, then poured in around the bolt. The lead was sometimes pounded in cold. The other sign was a recent one from nature—the skull of an Evening Grosbeak with only one eye socket, and the beak lying on the margin of ice beneath an overhanging jack pine. We guessed the poor little fellow must have been killed by some land animal—a little tragedy that happens every day out here. If we had been wearing boots, we wouldn't have bothered to travel the three miles of shoreline, but with skates and the ice near perfect, it was an effortless glide. Oh, we could have shot a puck a kilometre.

We returned to our shelter and the business at hand, which was to safely store the tarpaulin and stove and tidy up for when we'd be back in the spring. We hid the stuff, not to deny anyone protection and heat, but because we were a little bit leery of being spotted from the air and having our stuff destroyed. We were only doing what we considered a traditional thing—a right even—but if we got caught all they'd have to torch would be some poles. Paper companies mostly respect traditional uses of the Crown land they lease but we weren't taking any chances.

Just before we headed out, I found the remains of what appeared to be a table made of saplings between two trees. Nothing strange about this—just a common enough sign of some forerunner—so I thought no more of it until three or four years later when I was talking with a new acquaintance about my travels in this country and, in particular, this lake. He told me he used to go into the lake to fish, and that he and friends had built a lean-to there. Did I see any signs of this? No, but I mentioned the platform. Yep, that was his work alright, and this is his story.

There were four of them, two at the campsite, and he and another fishing further down the lake in a boat, when a helicopter appeared and hovered over the campsite. The four companions thought they were in for some kind of inspection. They watched warily as the chopper got lower and lower, when one of its crew began yelling down at the two fellows by the camp. The noise of the engine was so great they couldn't make out what he was saying. The chopper hovered, and a crewman threw something down at the campers. It was a vomit bag with a message written on it informing my friend that his mother had suddenly died, and that they were here to get him. Since they couldn't land there, they said they would land on the bog down on the big lake and wait for him. The helicopter was from the Department of Lands and Forests, and he was the only one they took out.

It was finally back to our cart on the big lake, and a lot lighter too. We got clear of the bog and put on our skates before we started off to another area of the lake and another job we had to take care of. It was a good thing our cart had a light load and that we could skate, because we were going to be covering about eight miles before finally returning to where we had put our tent the day before, and setting up camp. We were getting back our skating legs for sure on this trip! The objective now was to retrieve a steel outdoor fireplace another friend and I had stashed somewhere on Tangier Grand Lake three years before, and had forgotten about until my friend asked if, while on this trip, I would try to find it and take it to a site on the lake he and I had long used on fishing trips, and where we also had a fourteen-foot fibreglass boat.

Heading up and out of Southwest Cove with its broken shoreline and islands offered ordinary sights, like a spruce growing from a crack in a large granite boulder—a lesson in perseverance. Out here it's natural to look at simple things, I find, which is a pretty good indication of how nature puts the brakes to your racing brain, when you take the time to sit with her.

We knew for sure that there were moose in this country when I once saw one swimming just about where we were now. As we flowed alongside a bordering bog, we noticed a cranberry bog still harbouring droppings similar to a cow plop, with whole cranberries in them. I figured that moose had a problem when whole berries could go in one end and out the other without the least damage. At any rate, we were mighty glad to know that this land was still wild and remote enough to support moose.

This was freewheeling travelling; I've never experienced anything like it, and not likely ever will again. When we entered the main body of the lake we saw clean ice stretching off into the distance in every direction. We felt we had come upon some natural phenomenon that happens only when there's nobody there to see it—but here we were.

Since I had only a general idea where that fireplace was, and since looking a half mile across the lake to land that is only a solid dark band with no indication of coves, islands, or peninsulas, I could only guess in which direction to head. When we coasted up to the shore, I found myself fooled by one spot after another being the hiding place. The search required walking into the bushes, so I was back in my boots to do the scouting, while Briant cruised offshore. After about an hour I finally found the thing, so I hauled it out onto the ice. When I looked at it, I wondered what in the name of blazes I was doing carting this heavy hunk of iron around, but my friend thought we needed it, so Briant and I got to work. There was no better time than now, what with our cart, and the ice. We unloaded our cart except for some food and a burner, piled the stuff on the ice as a marker for our return, and loaded the fireplace on. Incidentally, removing your boots and putting on skates several times a day is a great way to trim the waistline. It didn't seem that hard forty years ago.

For the next two and a half miles we picked our way through a confusion of islands and great boulders rearing up out of the ice, when we finally reached the spot. This meant changing into our boots again to lug the iron contraption two hundred feet up a wooded knoll. When we reached the site the cache wasn't as I had left it; it was strewn all over the place. If a bear smells something good, then I can understand him rummaging through the stuff, but all there was here was a heavy canvas tent, some tools, some dry items and a bottle of spikes. Why that bear spread everything out when his nose told him not to bother was one thing, but biting through the plastic screw cap of the bottle of nails without crunching the glass was, to me, a pretty neat piece of work. It supported the idea I have that bears are afraid of glass so they never break it, although people have told me they've seen the work of bears breaking windows to get inside cabins. We had a lot of tidying up to do before we had a mug-up back on the ice. Sitting on a granite boulder overlooking the great expanse of ice reflecting the blue from a cloudless sky, with only the merest whiff of cold air on your face, clears your mind of life's problems and injects a magic potion into your innards that makes you feel so good. The thunder from the ice sent cracks speeding like bullets for a mile or more until they hit shore, and spoke of the wildness of the country we were lost in. Captivating as this was, we had to shake our mugs dry and start heading back.

We had time. There were things we wanted to see at this end of the lake, so we scooted along just about wherever we pleased, the near-empty cart rolling along with us. One feature we wanted to examine was a sand beach one-hundred-and-fifty-feet long, like you'd expect to find on an ocean shoreline; but the lake was open to the blast of winds from the north, always grinding the granite rocks to produce fine sand. It was a beautiful strip shelving out fifty feet before you're knee deep. The ice wasn't smooth right up to the sand, so we couldn't get close enough to identify tracks that littered the beach. Now it was back into our boots, because there were things on land we wanted to take a closer look at, the first being a small island that rose steeply out of the ice; we could see some sort of man's handiwork through the trees. It was an open and bare pole framework with a metal roof. Pieces of a stove were strewn around, and an iron cot just about filled the space, so this long-gone builder was probably a bit of a loner. He must have had to row ashore for firewood, because the island was so small that if he had used the trees there it would have been bald after two cold nights. I did pick up one item and took it with me—an unopened tin of kippers. Since then, Kipper Island has been a signpost to us, especially in the fog. (I opened the tin a year later—good as new!) By the time we got back to the pile of gear on the ice, it was late afternoon and time to get moving back to set up the tent.

When we got there the sun was a vivid rosy orange, streaking rays of colour across the ice through the treetops, and strangely, that fiery paint job looked so cold—it felt cold. We had a choice of putting up the tent on a nice spot alongside the old dam, or another good spot some two hundred feet away, but the spot near the dam was too noisy for quiet conversation, so we opted for another spot where we could still have the restful background noise of running water. We hadn't brought in the heavy metal poles for the tent, so we cut four poles, stood them pyramid fashion, and suspended the tent inside. There's lots to keep you busy getting comfortable for a cold February night in the woods. A warming fire, though, is a luxury you can't afford in very cold weather, because you have to expend too much energy keeping one going, so we just concentrated on hot food.

At last light, I was walking to the dam to fill two pots of water when I saw a mink slip silently into a hole in the ice—the only sign of life around, with not even a gray jay coasting in looking for a handout.

Living conditions now were not so easy as the night before, because all we had was our little burner to do the heating, but we soon filled our water bottles and threw them into our sleeping bags. It was dark now, but our two candle lanterns put out as much cheer as they could with the temperature at -23°C, which soon stiffened your fingers on bare-handed jobs, like pumping up the frigid naphtha burner time and again. The naphtha didn't seem to want to flow easily—the stuff was still fifty degrees away from its freezing point so if it wasn't turning to gel it was at least getting a bit stiff. Any discomfort you feel out here easily loses its grip once you look skyward on a clear, dark night like this; you become mesmerized by the startlingly spectacular spectacle you see only out here. If there's anything in this world you should stand in awe of, it's the clear nighttime winter sky above the woods. And that's what we last saw when we finally decided to turn in.

Crawling into our bags at eight o'clock, with our feet gripping the hot-water bottles, seemed a little early, but this was the only way to keep warm, and it was a darn sight more comfortable discussing the day's work this way, than crouched on the frozen ground in the dark with runny noses. What capped this day for us, and kept us awake in rapt attention for a long time, was the howling and yapping of coyotes far over some distant, dark hills; but they, as well as the sound of rushing water, eventually grew fainter as we slowly dozed off. What a way to go to sleep!

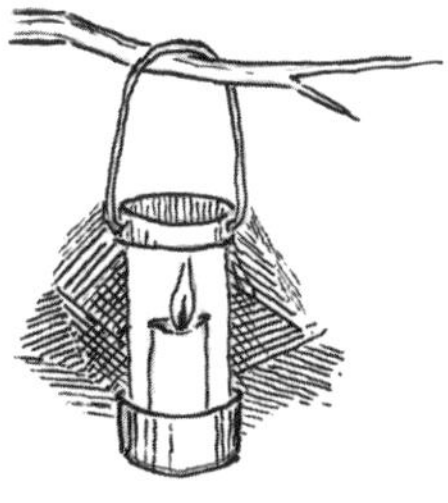

DAY THREE

No matter how many times you do it, to wake up warm and intact after a night under the frigid winter stars, gives you a bit of a start—gee, I made it! It was like that with this wake-up, with the frost from our breath built up on our balaclavas. It was still dark at six o'clock—we had slept for nine hours—so we lay in our warm cocoons for a half hour or so until it was light enough outside to see what you were doing. This is when you'll really see Murphy showing how his law works, and the choicest example of it I've ever experienced was at the expense of my trusty chum, when he thrust his arm out through the tent flap to empty his pee pot and, wouldn't you know it, his blind aim made a direct hit on my naphtha burner. If ever you saw a fellow wait patiently and humbly for his hot tea, it was him.

This day was free. All our tasks had been carried out, so we had the day to ourselves just to explore around—no rush to get anywhere, and at liberty to go there by foot. First it was a good hot breakfast, so oatmeal was the main dish, once the burner got rid of its dousing, flavoured, in Briant's case, with a liberal sprinkling or raisins. I threw a handful of chopped dates in mine, and after getting the molasses into a pouring state by immersing the plastic bottle into a saucepan of hot water, I spooned it over English muffins. That, with the hot tea, fixed us up for whatever the day could throw at us. Then it was into our skates and light backpacks, which held some food and our boots, and off we went, keen as kids going to the pond for a day of hockey.

The eastern reaches of Tangier Grand Lake are a maze of islands, peninsulas and coves, practically never touched by man because of the shallow, rocky waters without land access. The fourteenth largest lake in Nova Scotia, it is unique from the bigger ones, in that not a single road goes to it; the closest, a gradually deteriorating old hauling road, stops a third of a mile away, which reflects some sensitive woodland management, notably by the Prest brothers of Mooseland. In recent years, there have been four unauthorized cabins on the lake, but by the time of this visit, two had been removed at the request of the paper company that leased the surrounding land. Another one is an old derelict, pretty well messed up by bears, and so well hidden in its dilapidated state that it will not likely be seen by anyone except browsers like us who happen to chance by every two years or so. This lake is returning to the wild—surprising for this day and age, but the backwoods aren't attracting the numbers of fishermen and hunters it once did, no doubt due to newer pastimes of a changing society. That trend is welcomed by woods travellers who still like getting away from it all to where even a cellular phone won't work. That's fine with us.

Cruising around one island after another where there wasn't even a spot of open water was so effortless that you felt like you were being taken into tow by some magical force—the pure fun of it was magical for sure. Forerunners on our path, outside those provided by nature, would be appreciated, but that wasn't why we were here. All we wanted was the cold air on our faces and the privilege of being here.

We had to circle just about every island, sixteen or seventeen of them, simply because of the ease in doing it. On circling one of the larger ones, we noticed something through the trees we couldn't make out from the ice, so off came the skates and on went the boots—what a great workout our bellies were getting—to go check it out. It turned out to be another old lean-to sheathed with heavy black polyethylene. The roof was flat, not a very bright way to build a shelter, so the plastic was sagging heavily with ice, which I released with a few slashes of my knife. We took down the rotted poles and broke them up, then got a good fire going with some dead boughs and began piling on the plastic. The black smoke we created was unsightly, but getting rid of that bane of the backwoods brought in by people who couldn't care less, was a good feeling. Now, I didn't mean to bore you with something as uninteresting as tearing down an old lean-to, except that it made something catch my eye. Among the rusted tins and bottles lying around was an artifact that looked like it belonged to a long-gone age. Why it was in the company of modern-day plastic and people probably half my age, I'll never know. It was an old candle lantern, rusted and dented, with a stub of a candle still in it. The builders of the shelter either brought it in or came upon it at some old campsite. Actually, the thing looked like it might have been handmade, so maybe wasn't as old as it looked.

Tangier Grand Lake is so broken up with coves and peninsulas that its shoreline measures about twenty-one miles, every foot of which is studded with granite. We finally broke out of this confusion of rocks and islands, and entered a deep cove with a stream tumbling in. Here we entered the woods and followed the stream a short piece before coming out onto the lake we wanted to see—Rainy Lake. Here was a "lake of the woods" alright, absolutely quiet and surrounded by dense spruce. The ice was smoother than anything we'd been on so far, without any pressure ridges, but our skates were down on the big lake. Stepping out onto the ice in as pristine a setting as you could ever find, we felt like discoverers, and observed everything as we walked the shoreline, hoping we wouldn't find any traces of earlier visitors, and there wasn't a sign. This had to be a swell fishing spot, if you could get a boat up through the stream, and since it was unlikely that anyone would attempt such a haul, especially with the heavy boats needed on big lakes, there had to be lots of fish there. We had just about finished our skirt of the shoreline, when we entered a small cove near where we came in, and were astonished to find ourselves looking through open woods at the big lake—and a rusted and broken kerosene lantern hanging from a tree, and some logs to skid a boat through. Damned if we weren't discoverers after all! Our only consolation regarding these phantoms of the past was that they were unlikely to ever return. We returned to our skates and put them on to cover the five miles over ice back to our campsite.

Still morning, the low sun either blinded us or sent long

shadows across our path, depending on where the broken shoreline took us. Going from shadow to sunlight was passing from chilly to plain cold—and with no wind up, we glided from one shore feature to another, the only sound, apart from the cannonading of the ice off in the distance, being the cutting of our steel blades across the hard surface of the ice. After two miles of this effortless meandering, we decided to stop for lunch on a large, sloping boulder bathed in sunlight, where we removed our skates. We were enjoying the whole scene so much that we decided to make a little fire to melt ice for tea and warm our hands. A cooking fire fitted the picture far better than our little stove; even if it was more work, that was part of the fun of it, so we soon got some dead spruce blazing away in an indentation in the rock you'd swear was sculpted by a stonecutter for that purpose. We stretched out on the sloping granite, as the water heated in a pot we had slung from a stick held firmly by a slab of rock, deeply intoxicated by the purity of our surroundings, feeling like kids doing something exciting for the first time on their own.

On one of my short forays along the edge of the lake to gather firewood, I came upon the remains of some old pilings, about a foot high, forming what I took to be a dam. But, after studying it a bit, we realized it was a wall built to prevent the lake from spilling out into lower land when the water level was raised by the dam operators fifty years ago.

It was hard to leave our lunch spot in the sun and out of the wind, but it was too cold for sitting around, so it was back on with the skates again. We were in a large cove, a mile long, with a large island in the middle, which we wanted to circle, just to be able to say we did it, and because of the feeling of roaming free as the wind kept drawing us on. After we circled the island we returned to the mainland in the shadow of steeply rising forest, looming darkly above us. There was a cold north wind striking us from across the lake, so it wasn't much fun anymore. With the wind pushing against us it was more like work. We followed the straight line of brooding land for a mile along an inhospitable shoreline, where the trees came right to the water's edge to fend us off, so we headed north across the lake to our campsite and the end of our sojourn here.

Now it was cold! The wind was coming up strong in our faces, giving a wind chill of probably -30°C or more. We skated to beat the devil, every stride putting a hard thrust on the leg muscles. There was no talk now of sending a puck a mile; just getting into the shelter of the distant islands was all we desired. After a mile of shoving against the wind, we plopped ourselves down on the ice and took off the skates for the last time, finding it easier to stride along in our boots. As we approached the first island, we saw a bunch of crows flying around making one awful ruckus, so we slowed our pace, looking for whatever was getting them so riled up. Suddenly a snowy owl flew from the trees, beating a fast retreat to another island, the crows in hot pursuit, diving and swooping like World War I fighter planes. We saw only little of this forest drama because some open water in a narrow channel steered us in one direction, while the birds flew in another. The open water forced us to walk the shore of an island with only gnarled scrubby spruce and jack pine growing on it—not an inviting place—when something caught my eye. It was a short piece of rusted stovepipe around the trunk of a bushy little spruce tree. That whimsical fellow who put it there must have done so when the tree was very small, otherwise the pipe wouldn't have fit over it. A tough forerunner to figure out, that one!

By the time we got back to the tent, we needed some hot tea and food. Coaxing that cranky little burner into giving off a blue flame took some time, but finally we got something warm into us. Then we pulled up stakes. Off we trundled, darn glad for a job well done, and retraced our way through the pull-through to Bear Lake then across to the old hauling road. It was time, too, since it was getting on to late afternoon with dusk soon to follow. Our cleats were crunching into the ice but it was still slow going on these thirty-degree slopes. After only a mile down the road an overcast sky began to really darken things up—we'd be walking out after dark for sure.

The deep woods is a mysterious place; it has a lot of shadows and hiding places. Even the experienced woods traveller will sneak a peek over his shoulder once in a while when he's alone. The forest does something to the human mind—gets a hold on it and makes it think strange things. The darker and gloomier it is, the better it works, and that's why grand stories get told in woods cabins when a nice fire is crackling away in the stove.

I was taking my turn in the yoke with Briant pushing from the rear whenever he could get a grip on the ice with his cleats, when I noticed some movement up ahead at the crest of a hill. The light was now dim, so I passed it off as an illusion, and said nothing. We plugged on silently, more intent on beating the dark than anything else, when I thought I saw a figure at the far end of a level stretch. It disappeared around a bend, but now I mentioned it to my chum, who passed it off as my imagination. This disturbed me. I was seeing something—I've got a level head and I know what I see—yet I was starting to doubt myself. Well, damned if I wasn't determined to see whatever that was up ahead, so I rammed my cleats hard into the ice to get to the top of the next rise in a hurry. When I did, I spotted it! "There…there it is…can't you see that horse? That's a horse, for Christ sake…let's get up there an' see what's goin' on," I yelled, urging Briant to push harder. All I got from him were some choice words telling me to get a hold on myself. So I did, and now it became clear to me. I wasn't seeing things—I was seeing Fraser Prest's horse. That was Fraser's horse that got so riled up by the blackflies while waiting to take out some sports in May 1939, that he took off in desperation to Mooseland, and the safety of his barn.

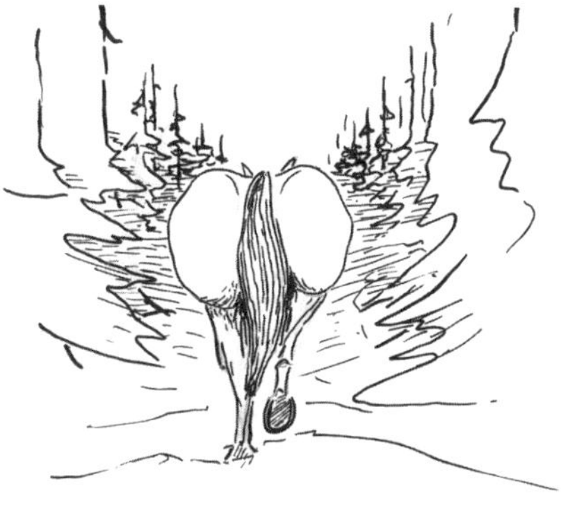

After a January thaw

DAY ONE

A half mile in, we unburdened ourselves of our snowshoes because there wasn't enough snow on the trail to bother with. We'd pick up the six shoes, stuck in some deep snow off the path, on our return the next day. There had been a January thaw and some rain so we guessed our seven miles in would be mostly icy where we'd be on land, which would be about half the time. The ever-present ice cleats dangling and clinking from one of the buckles on our backpacks were at the ready, and it was certain by the look of things that they'd come in handy before long.

The early morning sky was bright enough to light the way and an hour or so would see the cold shafts of sunlight streaking long shadows from the spruce trees across our route. We made our way silently because that always seems to be the way you should move through the early-morning woods, when you never know what you might come upon, and what you hope you can surprise. Single file, we wended our way along the long-unused hauling road, which was getting narrower. The wonder of it was that thirty years or more ago, we used to drive in the whole two and a half miles to the first lake—and with a boat on top at that. Now it was getting to be a woods trail again, which we liked very much.

A milestone can be just what it says, except this milestone was a stony stream. When you are heading for a milestone, carrying a heavy load on your back, it seems to take an awfully long time to reach it. But when you do reach it, the load seems to get lighter. And that's just the way we felt when we stopped at that stream heavy with water from the recent rains. We paused for a rest, and studied which ice crowned rock was least likely to dump you in the water when you stepped on it.

The stream here emptied into a stillwater bordered on one side by heavy woods, and on the other by a wide expanse of bog where the grass had long since been cut short by winter's work. The recent mild spell had opened up part of the water and the rains had flooded the remaining ice, making it smoother and darker, leaving us to wonder what we'd find ahead on the two lakes we'd be crossing. Once across the stream, we found that the road had been washed mostly clean of snow and ice, so there was no need to put on the ice cleats. Following along with us were the prints of coyote and wildcat in the frozen slush. For most of its length, the road is like the bed of a rocky stream, and we could imagine that it ran just like a regular brook after heavy rains and a spring melt, funnelling away water from the higher surrounding ground. With conditions like this, there'd be no hope of the lead man coming face to face with a coyote, because there was thick snow cover to muffle your footsteps, and any other noises you make. We knew this, so had picked up our conversation a ways back, still in hushed tones—like when sightseeing in an empty church.

We continued on our way, sometimes under a canopy of boughs of old growth spruce, then under blue sky where the trees were younger and more spaced out. It was somewhere along this stretch that a man who knew the area well had pointed out to me a blackened stump of a tree, which I discovered to be charcoal. He told me it was the remains of a fire that swept through there in 1949. It was hard to believe that you could still get charcoal off a tree stump after forty-five years of exposure to the elements. I mentioned this to Briant and Vaughn, but was unable to spot any blackened stumps because of the snow cover.

When we reached the first lake, we were not surprised to see the problem we expected—newly frozen-over spots that would cause us to detour and slow us down. Old ice and new—the black ice that doesn't show its thickness by trapped bubbles or cracks—was bare of any snow. This was good because it made for easier walking without the fear of a foot slipping, which happens when there is a light dusting of snow or when snow sticks to your sole. We just had to watch for thin ice and keep to the grey ice. A test hole chopped through the new ice showed only about two inches, not nearly enough to walk on, so that scotched the temptation of taking a shorter route to the end of the lake. Stepping up onto the low bog at the end, we took a short pull-through to the big lake where we stopped to make tea and have lunch.

Sitting on the gunwale of a rowboat half submerged in ice, and enjoying our lunch out of the wind, our talk centred on how peaceful it was so far from all the stuff that goes on "back there," and how it was too bad that more people couldn't be "out here" to get the right slant on things. No room for pretension out here. I'll always remember those moments sitting on that derelict boat because of a swell quote from Vaughn: "When the game is over, the king and the pawn go back in the same box."

We couldn't see the three miles we'd have to travel across this lake from our rest spot because of the intervening islands and peninsulas, so we were anxious to be off to see what lay ahead. We aimed between two islands, but when we got there we found our way blocked by open water, so we took solid ice to the island on our right, and walked its shore until we came to solid ice again. We groped around like this for an hour, all the while being driven away from the direction we wanted to take by wide expanses of treacherous black ice. Hugging the main shoreline of the lake, we finally saw, leading off across the main body of the lake, a distinct boundary between black ice and grey ice—our route to get back on track again. Once across here, we'd be on thicker ice for the last mile down a large branch of the lake.

Walking that dividing line between a good dunking and safety was something worth experiencing. A few blows of the hatchet a few feet out from where you were standing would bring water boiling up, while at your feet the ice was too thick to get through. It was a good thing, we commented, that we weren't making this trip in a blizzard.

Finally across the widest part of the lake, we entered the southwest branch. Here there was no black ice; it hadn't opened up during the thaw. Clear blue sky, sun's glare off the ice sometimes blinding, just a light wind—the perfect ingredients of a tonic guaranteed to lighten the heart, and cause involuntary exclamations, "...my geez, this is beautiful." But coming to a large island halfway down the branch, I was forced to make a visit and told the boys to carry on; I'd catch up. I watched them get smaller and smaller until it was almost as if they had passed out of my life altogether. Alone. All of a sudden alone in that big country, near to getting the jitters in case something should go wrong.

For me, winter gives off as much, if not more, colour than springtime flowering (like the purple rose rhodora around a lake's edge), or autumn hues. This is largely due to the bending of light—ice crystals are tiny prisms. The shows of colour may be tiny but they are brilliant! Constant flashes from the whole spectrum catch your eye when the sun is shining and creates a spectacle far flashier that the steady colour of the blue flag iris. Since I was on the boys' trail, I relaxed a bit, and wandered over to a snowbank along the forest's edge to prod it with my staff (a third leg which often comes in handy). I enlarged the hole to see the pale aqua-marine glow light up the hole which always happens when there's plenty of light; there doesn't have to be bright sunlight for this phenomenon. Why nature sends out this particular glow from the lower end of the spectrum instead of the red, oranges and yellows, I don't know, but it always does. The frigid fastness of the winter woods can dazzle the eye like no other I know.

It was over six miles by now, slow ones at that, and early afternoon. I was glad when I picked up foot prints into the woods. With a half mile to go, I could soon chuck my pack and relieve my feet at our campsite. Here I'll confess to our temporary A-frame of spruce poles situated on Crown land leased to a paper company—though not legal, this is tolerated. We were repeating a practice that had continued for the last century and a half, but we didn't build permanent camps like the two in this area that had been torched by the builders at the request of the paper company. The area we were travelling is a provincial protected area.

Moose Tree Lodge was a fitting name for our simple abode because of a dead spruce tree on the site that had a gnarled top almost exactly in the shape of a moose's head. Similar to the A-frame mentioned earlier, Moose Tree Lodge had a few extra refinements. Two sapling platform bunks were thickly padded with moss; there was a drying rack above our little sheet metal stove, and a shelf next to the stove made a handy storage place. Polyethylene still covered the structure after a November trip in. The boys' packs were there, but the boys weren't; they were back in the woods retrieving some gear hidden from the bears but apparently, as it turned out, not from man. The boys soon arrived with some things, but only one sleeping bag. Somebody had spied the blue bundle used to store two sleeping bags eight feet up a tree, and helped themselves to one. The guy must have been desperate, so we didn't begrudge him taking one; however, this left poor Vaughn literally out in the cold, since it was his bag that was gone. We had two bags, Briant's and mine, which I brought in, but they weren't doubles, as would normally be the case when sleeping in a tent with no stove. I kept reminding the two that it wasn't my idea to wrap the gear in a bright blue tarp for all the world to see against the dark spruce and snow. Storing the gear high up a thin tree might keep bears from rummaging around before the winter's onslaught, but it's man you've got to be thinking about in the woods, not bears.

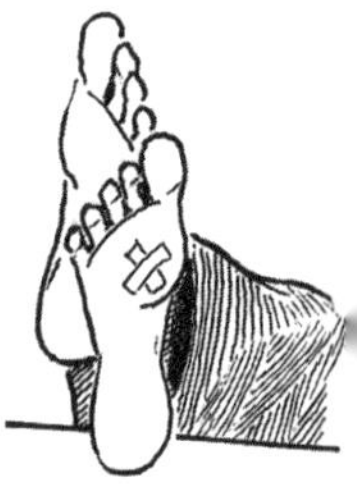

Sitting in that shelter nestled against a hill with a sunny western exposure, eating lunch and drinking hot tea was one enjoyable respite. The boots were off, even. We repaired the plastic, where a bear had clawed a couple of holes, with the ever-present duct tape, and planned the rest of the day. Telling your family you're going overnight in the woods in February has to be justified somehow so we always have to cook up some story or other. This one was that two guys we knew had wooden boats in need of repairs on three lakes in here. They were getting too old to make a winter trip in here like they used to, so could we tend the boats? The truth is that they never asked us any such thing, but we were sure they'd appreciate it if we did the work and so there's the truth. We were in to repair boats we never use. Why not say that we make these trips for the good of our health?

Off we went, with some food and two cans of plastic cement. A mile up, we found one boat, did the work, then skirted a run up to another lake and did the next one. By now it was getting on to sundown so we had to give up on the third boat because it was too far away. Stopping at the run on our way back, we got some water for tea and sat on the rocks. Talk turned to how it was safer travelling in threes than twos; two could carry an injured man out whereas one man couldn't. Then we belaboured the obvious—that the first priority in woods travel was to keep dry, the second was to keep warm, with food placing a distant third. Finally, we had a pretty good discussion on such topics as the surface tension of water, the wicking capacity of wool compared to cotton, and about whether it was less dangerous, barring drowning, to fall into the water on a cold winter day, or during wet weather in early spring.

All three of us had our experiences with falling in, but it was agreed that falling into icy water, up to your thighs or waist, was not nearly so miserable as doing the same thing on a drizzly day in spring. This, of course, supposes that you don't get in front of a hot stove in a cozy cabin any time soon. On a cold winter day, the water freezes on your clothing—assuming you are wearing heavy wool pants—so the ice actually insulates your body. The water doesn't wick up through the rest of your clothing either. I've experienced this, and have sometimes had to walk miles before getting to some shelter. In wet weather in early spring, the water wicks up to your midriff, and if there's anything that'll chill you to the bone, getting you darn near to serious hypothermia, that's it. It was Briant who one time gave me relief from uncontrollable shivering after a wet day fishing on a lake in our rain gear. Sitting before a fire with my rain clothes still on, I couldn't stop shivering no matter how close I got to the fire. Briant said to take the rain gear off and the moment I did my body relaxed. My rain pants and jacket had been holding in all the dampness from moisture and sweat. It was as easy as that. As for wool compared to cotton in keeping you more comfortable when you're wet, that's one for the physicists. For some reason your hands don't get cold in wet woolen mitts, but they will with most other materials. On this trip, the wool mitts I was wearing were knitted by a man who kindly asked me to send him an outline of my hand on a piece of paper so he could knit me a pair of mitts. They are 50/50 mohair and sheep wool. Lee Bushell is an experienced woodsman so I didn't doubt him when he advised me that the mittens might shrink a bit from snow water.

Once the cold sun had dipped below the spiky dark outline of spruce along the western horizon, it got noticeably colder. We made our way back to our cold abode in the gloom of the woods, but we'd soon get the little stove roaring, and see just how good it was on its first winter test in this spot.

Even though you're huddling in the dark at six o'clock in the evening around the stove, getting it going and shedding some light on the subject, it still doesn't make for a long night, since your evening generally ends at nine o'clock anyway—when you work yourself into your sleeping bag and that blessed envelope of warmth. We did get a good fire going in the stove, and two candle lanterns gave enough light to see what we were doing. We also discussed at length, over tea and beans heated on our little iosol stove, who was going to sleep on the narrow piece of ground between the two bunks, and especially how Vaughn was going to keep warm through the night, since he was the one who drew the bad hand on this outing.

The candle lanterns lent our cabin some cheer, but the heat from the stove was mostly dispersed into the surrounding darkness. The polyethylene didn't hold it in very well, nor did the opening around where the stovepipe went out, but it was better than nothing. Vaughn deserved a soft bunk, naturally, and I drew the wrong number and got assigned to the floor.

Our first concern was Vaughn. Briant and I tucked him in with our heavy jackets—usually our favourite pillows—then we laid our two thin sponge sleeping pads over him and clamped them in place with spring clamps we used to close the flaps at the doorway. At -15°C, you need a good sleeping bag to hold in the heat but Vaughn didn't have that luxury. I had it a lot warmer than he did, even though I had no padding, just some plastic and newspaper as insulation between me and the ground, and some bunched up odds and ends for a pillow. You keep your pants on at times like this. With only a seven-inch square opening, the little stove couldn't hold enough wood for a good fire, and neither Briant nor I could face the discomfort of struggling out of our bags to keep shoving wood in the stove through the night so the stove soon held only dying embers. Vaughn didn't fare too well through the night and though, by comparison, Briant and I had it pretty good, morning couldn't come soon enough for the three of us.

DAY TWO

Once you get a fire going and some hot tea into you, it's like you took an upper. Bundled up again in your clothes and moving around, you gradually warm up but when the sun's rays start shooting in horizontally through the tree tops, that's what really gets the juices flowing to tackle another day. Today was one going to be spent, first, fixing up the campsite, then clearing away some debris that was choking up a run to a favourite fishing hole of ours.

The first chore was to relocate the hiding spot. We stashed some of the gear in a spot where the water begins to make an exit from the lake, and where no one would ever think to set foot. That done, we had some fun discussing little conveniences that would make our next stay here a bit more comfortable. We stuffed firewood under the bunks, along with all the bark from a long-rotted birch tree I came across further back in the woods. That amazing stuff, soaked like it is with oil of wintergreen, never rots. With all the housekeeping done, we shut the draught on the stove and proceeded to our next task.

There was a cove about half a mile from our campsite that led into a long, narrow bog with a narrow stream running out of a bowl-like lake, perhaps five hundred feet away. This was our early spring fishing haven. We figured that breeding trout went up into this lake in the fall, because we would always catch big fish there in the spring in a deep hole that we had discovered.

This secluded little lake had no visible supply of water so it had to be spring fed; somewhere at the bottom of the hole was a spring welling up through a hard, gravelly bottom—ideal for spawning and rearing young trout. It was during one of those quite moments in the woods that you luck into seeing something you ordinarily wouldn't. I was once sitting on the bank of the boggy run draining this little lake, with my feet dangling in the water, when what should parade past me but a line of young trout, each about three inches long. I could've been the stump of a tree for all they knew. This might seem like a small matter but it was a thrill for me and, of course, it confirmed our suspicion that the hole was indeed a prime breeding spot.

While in our "hot spot" the previous spring, we caught the usual large trout but had noticed a solid blockage of the little run. We didn't know whether or not fish could pass through it somehow, perhaps during a freshet, but we decided to clear it anyway. Since we weren't wearing rubber boots, we had to work from both sides of the bank. Briant cut a pole, leaving the butt of a limb at the end, which acted as a hook, and with this we were able to clear the whole obstruction. There were a lot of branches stripped of bark, indicating that beavers were at work close by, although they hadn't actually worked at this spot. Our labours probably didn't make a bit of difference to whether or not fish passed along this route; how often had this steam been blocked over a thousand years, yet cleared itself so fish could continue using it? Anyway, we had come to this hidden spot in remote country, locked in the icy grip of winter, yet with pitcher plant still erect (although now holding only ice) and with cranberries hanging on for some browser to come along, more to enjoy its natural history than to clear a clogged run. Still, we were glad we cleared the dam, and satisfied ourselves that the big breeders would once again have easy passage into our secret place.

Most of this run was frozen over—you could walk on it in places—and it was while I was poking around that I came upon a spot of ice as clear as glass. It gave an undisturbed view of the bottom, and you couldn't help but peer down through this window to see if anything was moving. And there sure was. Not fish, but insects. Thank heaven for the way that water expands, which I've mentioned earlier. Without that miracle of nature, there would be no life in waters after freeze-up, because the water would freeze from the bottom up instead of from the top down. The bottom of this stream must have been teeming with life, for through this small window two whirligigs caught my eye. Those two tiny black beetles weren't scooting around crazily like you see them do on the surface of water but seemed to be very deliberate in their movements. No doubt they were looking for food, but the coldness of the water would have slowed them down as well. They breathe by trapping air on their bodies. Since there is only one generation per year, adults overwinter to lay their eggs in early spring. No sooner had I caught sight of these whirling dervishes than what should pass by but a backswimmer, looking like he was using a pair of oars, or a water boatman—I'm not sure which. To top it off, moving slowly over some small stones was a caddisfly larva encased in plant debris and looking like a small twig. This insect is familiar to fishermen in the spring, when it gets the trout all stirred up looking for nymphs. All this life in early February!

The three of us headed back to the campsite to remove the plastic from the A-frame and pack up. It was now around two o'clock and with seven miles to get to the truck, we wouldn't have too much time for sightseeing if we wanted to get out before dark.

When we got back down to the big lake and started to

cross the ice, we came upon deer tracks on the occasional little drifts of snow. That deer had had a tough time walking on that hard ice because you could see where it had slipped several times, and once it was obvious where all four legs had gone out from under it. It seemed strange for a deer to venture out on smooth ice, and we laughed at the comical sight it must have been. As we continued walking, one of the guys spied something on the snow on the far shore of the cove. Here we went, sightseeing again! As we approached this unusual sight, we saw it was a bloody blotch, and those slipping and sliding hooves now told a story that there was nothing funny about it. There wasn't much left of it but, strangely, more than coyotes usually leave. The act probably took place before we passed that way the day before, because the blood didn't seem fresh—then maybe we had disturbed the drama, with the coyotes having left the remains until the all-clear was given to move back in again.

Sometimes together, sometimes with one straying away, we trudged on, Vaughn's eyes often falling shut as he walked, thinking of nothing in particular but feeling good in every fibre of our being from whatever it is out here that affects us this way. We might have made an interesting sight for anyone watching us from behind a tree, or up in some eyrie with a pair of binoculars. No snowmobiles here, and no designer labels either. This was a passage through elemental nature—that kind of nature that can bore into your gut, and make you smile at just about anything. We were so innocuous that we felt a part of the ice, rocks and trees. When you start thinking that way, you have transported yourself back to simpler times, when it was possible to separate yourself from man's dreary propensity for self-aggrandizement, which always becomes an affliction on others.

Captain William Chearnley, a British Army officer, roamed around the woods of this province in the mid-nineteenth century and had he been here with us, he would have felt just as he did back then. Our clothing would have caught his eye, though. He would have carried a blanket as a bedroll instead of my sleeping bag, and probably would have said mine was a better rig. We wouldn't have been able to show him caribou tracks like he was used to tracking, but he sure would have felt right at home had we come across some moose tracks. Briant and I could have shown him where we saw a moose swimming just the previous spring. He was a man more accustomed than us to facing privation, and he always carried his blanket across his back because, "when in the wilds it is hard to say where you may be obliged to pull up for the night."

On this wide expanse of ice I found myself separated from the boys, and I actually got into a conversation with Chearnley. His manner of speech was similar to mine, but some of his expressions had a nicer ring to them than those we would use. He had great tales to tell about hunting caribou and moose, and fishing salmon and trout. He recounted that once in 1840 when he and his Indian guide Joe Pennall, whom he called "a hunter of celebrity," were calling a moose, Joe was surprised and nearly run down by one coming up behind him. Joe's gun misfired three times so in desperation he flung his powder horn at the animal, hitting it on the antlers which caused it to make off.

Chearnley's escapades ran from somewhere between 1839 and the 1860s. When on a ten-day leave from his regiment in the spring of 1839, it took him a whole day to travel from Halifax to Musquodoboit River. With seven days of fishing, Sunday not being a fishing day either because of some religious belief he held, or because of some regulation, he caught forty-eight salmon, the largest, weighed by Mr. Crawford, proved to be thirty-three pounds.

When I listened to his tales coloured with terms like "barren jade," "loup cervier," and "rampike," I knew that here was a man who lived for the sporting life. I couldn't fully understand his need to take back "...a good bag to Halifax, 2 moose 1 carriboo & 1 bear," from the Dollar Lake area until he explained that the meat was used by the mess. He hit a familiar note with me when he complained about how all the mill dams were preventing salmon from moving up the rivers to spawn, and that there was no authority to stop them. I told him he shouldn't complain—he didn't know the half of it. I mentioned seeing deer tracks back on the big lake, and he commented that he wasn't surprised about that deer slipping and sliding. He explained how a caribou's hooves were designed to manage "glare ice," and recounted he once saw, in Guysborough county in the 1850s, a herd of eleven caribou scale a forty-five degree bank of sheer river ice with no trouble at all. He said their hooves have sharp edges that grip slick ice, and that they can expand their hooves to get bette footing, abilities that "...the moose or even the common deer don't have." It surprised me to hear him mention deer, as I thought they had vanished from Nova Scotia long before his time and that they had only begun re-populating the province in the 1870s. He was surprised to hear me say that.

I was so deep in my thoughts I suddenly found myself wandering onto that black ice, so I veered toward the boys who were aiming to a shoreline we'd have to follow for safety. After two days of walking, I was getting foot sore, even though my boots gave me more support than Chearnley's moccasins, which were almost always wet.

I avoided the tumble of granite for the smooth surface of the bordering new ice, and promptly broke through to my knees before grabbing onto a boulder where Vaughn gave me a hand. Just like we talked about the day before! The temperature was about -15°C, so my pants were soon frozen stiff, but that insulated my wet underclothing. My well-insulated footware soon warmed up the water inside, keeping my feet warm and lubricated to boot. The only drawback was that I was lugging more weight. There wasn't much sense in stopping to put on a pair of dry socks, since my boot liners were soaked so I just put up with it. Just keep moving.

William Chearnley rarely travelled the outdoors through the late spring and summer. The most pleasure he got travelling was bundling up under moose-skin blankets with his guide Joe in an ox-drawn sleigh, embarking from Halifax, taking a steam ferry across the harbour to Dartmouth, then making an overnight trip to the Musquodoboit or even getting as far as St. Mary's River. The overnight lodging was either with a hardy Scot settler friend, George Tulloch, or with an Indian friend of Joe's in his bare, one-room cabin. Once in the woods he and Joe would set up a waterproof canvas, soaked earlier with boiled oil and dried in the sun, slung over a horizontal pole. He called this a camp, not a tent. More often, he would stay in a cabin Chearnley himself had built. With some seventeen built either by himself or by Indian friends, ranging from the "Ingraham River" to the Stewiacke area and along the Guysborough Road as far as St. Mary's River, he had plenty to choose from. It's clear he was often better housed than we were. Apart from how we transported ourselves, once in the woods we were doing things pretty much the same as Chearnley, and certainly the scenery was unchanged from his day. He commented that on just about this spot he had returned to the woods to retrieve a moose he had shot the previous day to find a mink gnawing at the side of the animal: "I fired a bullet at the cad but I missed him." The larder for the mess got well stocked after this trip with Chearnley bringing back seven moose.

More than once, Chearnley hailed the woods of Nova Scotia for the spiritual uplift he got from its primeval vastness compared to the tight confines of the British Isles. He was a favoured gentleman, owning a schooner, which he sailed to different parts on hunting and fishing expeditions, but the Nova Scotia woods captivated him. And so it does us, not much different today than from his day. The three of us wondered if we were up to suffering privation like Chearnley did and predictably came to the conclusion that we were. Physical needs aside, it was clear all around with us, as with Chearnley, that icy winter travel does something to the soul, putting you into a great frame of mind that miraculously medicates you innards—something like a purgative.

Dog-tired, me somewhat miserable, we parted company with Chearnley back on the trail, got out at dusk and back to reality.